The Non-Objective World Revisited

1 July - 15 October 1988

Annely Juda Fine Art

11 Tottenham Mews (off Tottenham Street)
London W1P 9PJ

tel 01-637 5517   fax 01-580 3877
Mon – Fri: 10 am–6 pm   Sat: 10 am–1 pm or by appointment

Cover: Otto Freundlich, Abstract Composition   *c.* 1939, pastel on paper,   48.5 × 42 cm

ISBN 1 870280 09 1

©Annely Juda Fine Art, London   1988

Printed by Creasey Flood Ltd, Tower Road, Lowestoft, England

Albers · Arp · Bergmann-Michel · Bill · Calder · Chashnik
Ermilov · Exter · Francis · Freundlich · Gabo · Graeser · Held
Hepworth · Hinterreiter · Hoch · Honegger · Hughes · Kliun
Klucis · Kupka · Laurens · van der Leck · Leger · El Lissitzky
Lohse · Malevich · K. Martin · M. Martin · McLaughlin
Michel · Moholy-Nagy · Moore · Morellet · Pevsner · Poliakoff
Popova · Reynolds · Ribemont-Dessaignes · Schwitters
de Stael · Stazewski · Suetin · Tatlin · Vantongerloo
Vezelay · Vordemberge-Gildewart

Installation, The Non-Objective World 1914-1924, June–September 1970

It is just 10 years since we made our last 'Non-Objective World' exhibition. We thought it was a good moment to revisit the exhibition but extend into the Eighties and show some of the younger artists who still work in this tradition.

We are most grateful to all our friends and colleagues who helped to make this exhibition possible, amongst them the Hannah Hoch Estate, Ivor Braka, Nina and Graham Williams, Fischer Fine Art, Edward Totah, Waddington Galleries and Galerie Renée Ziegler. Last but not least, all the artists.

Annely and David Juda
June 1988

Installation, The Non-Objective World 1914-1939, June–September 1978

The Non-Objective World

A title like 'The Non-Objective World', which has already proved its usefulness in a series of group exhibitions at this gallery, still seems to me to be as good as any other, and considerably better than many that might be chosen in its place. Any combination of terms involving the word 'abstract' carries with it a host of problems, ranging from the inevitable Philistine response to the more informed (but ultimately fruitless) protests of the artists themselves, from Kandinsky and Arp onwards, who argued that their work was involved with the 'concrete' rather than its apparent opposite. Yet 'concrete', despite van Doesburg's 1930 manifesto and despite the general adherence of Swiss post-war artists to this term, has never gained any measure of general acceptance with the public, let alone the artists concerned. The same point applies to any variant on the concept of 'construction', whose historical and aesthetic significance has always tended to be particularised, even exclusive, rather than indicative of a wide spectrum of activity.

'The Non-Objective World' then has the advantage of being, quite unambiguously, the coinage of one particular artist, and thus of being located historically in a particular time and place. But Malevich's notion can also be extended, as a kind of synecdoche, to all the multifarious strands of activity which related, and still relate, to the non-figurative art of the Modern Movement. The term does not seek to define these strands of activity, let alone colonise them for one particular artistic ideology. It is like a flag flying at the masthead. The message is not exclusive.

Further thoughts on the relation of these works to history follow from this choice of a term. Here is an exhibition which includes work by a living artist, Henryk Stazewski, who knew in his formative years what it was like to feel the gravitational force of the two dominant idioms of Modernist painting – who felt, like his other Polish colleagues in the *Blok* group, the attraction of Mondrian's grid-like structures as well as that of Malevich's visionary space. Yet this is also an exhibition

in which several of the more recent artists feel no special allegiance to either idiom. Several, indeed, would see the East not in terms of the counterpoint to European, Post-Renaissance art provided by the example of Russian Modernism (a counterpoint deriving, as Norbert Lynton has suggested in a previous catalogue introduction, from the Byzantine, iconic tradition), but in terms of a more far-reaching Orientalism. John McLaughlin, for example, used the negation of Zen philosophy to underscore a use of abstraction that was deliberately non-rationalistic.

A host of other examples could be provided to show that, in this company, the exceptions vastly outweigh the rule. History in the sense of a coherent, causally explicable tradition is only to be found through a kind of wish-fulfilment. Malcolm Hughes' lozenge-shaped sequences can, if we choose, be related to the well-known example of Mondrian, and even to the intermediate example of Bolotowsky. But what is taking place within these works is likely to be obscured, rather than illuminated by such a connection. It would be clarified, perhaps, by a close attention to the way in which colour has been used, subject to a 'law' or rational procedure, in the life-work of Richard Paul Lohse, as well as by readings in the philosophical implications of colour naming, in the debate which was launched by Wittgenstein. But the perceptual effect of such colour contrasts and juxtapostions, however much it may be sanctioned by such a philosophical project, remains fresh and unpredictable.

This is not, however, to set up the principle of physical presence, or the immediacy of the work, in opposition to the notion of tradition, or the deferment of the work through an infinite series of formal correlations. What I would claim, in fact, as the appropriate alternative to a historical reading of 'The Non-Objective World', is a reading which takes account of the strategic insertion of art discourse into the present situation. Here it becomes more clear than ever that such work is not in any way the exhausted rear-guard of an early assault on the

Academy. Its critical force remains undiminished, indeed it has been accentuated by recent developments in the war of styles.

A brief comparison may make this point more comprehensible. In the 1960's, art of the 'abstract', 'concrete' or 'constructive' tendency thrived on the overdue reaction to the prevalent Expressionist styles of the immediate post-war period, as well as on the temporary eclipse of a strong figurative, academic art. The strategy of the *Nouvelle Tendance,* for example, was to favour an aesthetic of 'instability', in which the spectator's physiological capacities were exploited to the greatest possible degree. The *Groupe Recherche d'Art Visuel,* in particular, enunciated a radically reductive programme in which the 'eye' alone, divorced from cognition and cultural preconceptions, was to be the focus of their experiments. Morellet, a refugee from this group who is showing in the present exhibition, made an early and necessary recovery from a commitment that doomed most of his colleagues to artistic extinction.

The message is plain. No artist, not even a non-figurative artist, can wipe the slate clean of every other form of cultural conditioning. The 'eye' that sees this exhibition is an eye that has also witnessed the growth, and the widespread public display, of the works of the Neo-Expressionist movement. Does this mean that the 'Non-Objective World' is overwhelmed by sheer weight of bombardment? Certainly not. In fact, the converse is true. Just as one extreme engenders its opposite, so (in my view) the hyperactive pictorialism of the new schools actually strengthens the effect of works which abide by a very different rationale.

In fact, the real casualty of the 1980's has not been the domain of 'The Non-Objective World', but the simplistic and spontaneous abstract painting that developed in the wake of Expressionism and once appeared (in the English context, at any rate) to have become a well-nigh universal orthodoxy. The more rigorous art represented here confronts the newly burgeoning mythologies from a restricted, but carefully maintained high ground, whilst the old spontaneity collapses into a morass of its own making.

This may seem a priggish way of defending the type of art represented here. But it is important to underline the fact that we are no longer, in any sense, at the Bauhaus stage, or indeed at a stage represented by that renewal of didactic commitment which marked the 1960's. No one is likely to claim any longer that abstraction provides a universal method for the eliciting of form and structure, in the plastic arts as well as in design and architecture. But something of hardly less significance can, and must be claimed. This is that the art of 'The Non-Objective World' has a privileged connection with the contemporary discourses that form the spectrum of the human sciences. It is no accident that the issues connected with the philosophical status of colour are being investigated both by philosophers and by artists. Nor is it surprising that the issues arising around the theme of 'deconstruction' – which, with Derrida's blessing, have been carried over into the fields of architecture and the plastic arts –have struck a responsive chord among the younger artists working in the abstract, constructive area.

The 'Non-Objective World' is therefore not, in any way, a solipsistic world. It may forego the possibilities of direct representation. But it remains akin, in its epistemological procedures, to other modes of investigation –philosophical, mathematical, even sociological. Even if it does not borrow from them in the sense of taking over existing forms, it declares its kinship when it makes a concrete object to testify to a process of investigation. At that point, of course, there is never any easy short cut in the labour of realisation. Since the Renaissance, when Western painters perhaps began their close identification with the scientific spirit, it has been evident that art requires a supplement beyond science: in the words of Alberti, 'a more plump Minerva'.

Stephen Bann
Canterbury
May 1988

Josef Albers

Born Bottrop, Germany 1888. 1913-20 studied Konigliche Kunstschule, Berlin; Kunstgewerbeschule, Essen, Academy Munich. 1920-23 Bauhaus, Weimar. 1923-33 Master at the Bauhaus Weimar and Dessau. 1933-49 Professor Black Mountain College, Beris, North Carolina. Harvard University, Cambridge, Mass. 1949-50 Yale University, New Haven, Pratt Institute, Brooklyn. 1934-36 Member of 'Abstraction-Création', Paris. Since 1938 member of the 'American Abstract Artists'. 1953 and 1955 visiting lecturer Hochschule fur Gestallung, Ulm. 1955 Documenta 1, Kassel; 1956 Yale University, New Haven. 1961 Stedelijk Museum, Amsterdam. 1964 Museum of Modern Art, New York. 1965 Washington Gallery of Modern Art. 1968 Bauhaus Exhibition Stuttgart and London; Documenta 4, Kassel. 1970 Kunsthalle Hamburg. 1971 Metropolitan Museum of Art, New York. 1976 Died at New Haven, Connecticut, U.S.A.

1 Homage to the Square 1952
oil on masonite
56 × 56 cm
initialled and dated lower right

Jean Arp

Born 1887 in Strasbourg. 1904-1908 Studied at The School of Decorative Arts (l'école des Arts Décoratifs) Weimar and then at the Académie Julian, Paris. 1909 Meeting with Paul Klee. 1912 Met Wassily Kandinsky. Moved to Zurich in 1915. Exhibited collages and tapestries at the Galerie Tanner and met Sophie Täuber and in collaboration with her produced embroidery, carpets, tapestries and collages. 1916-1919 Co-founder of the Dada movement in Zurich with Hugo Ball, Tristan Tzara, Richard Huelsenbeck and others. 1919 Met Max Ernst in Cologne and took part in the Dada movement there. 1922 Married Sophie Täuber. 1922-1925 Worked on several art reviews: Schwitters' *Merz,* H. Walden's *Der Sturm,* Theo van Doesburg's *Mecano-De Stijl* and Hans Richter's *G.* Produced with Lissitzky 'Les Ismes dans l'Art'. 1925 Took part in the first Surrealist exhibition in Paris. 1926-1930 Member of the Surrealist group in Paris. Lived in Meudon from 1926 onwards. Designs for the Café 'Aubette' in Strasbourg together with Sophie Täuber-Arp and Theo van Doesburg. 1930-1934 Member of the groups 'Cercle et Carré' and 'Abstraction-Création'. 1931-1932 First sculpture. 1940-1945 In Grasse with Sonia Delaunay and Alberto Magnelli, then travelled to Zurich and Basle. 1946 Returned to Meudon. First complete French language edition of his poems 'Le Siège de l'Air'. Died 1966 in Meudon.

2 Untitled   1917-45
original woodcut from the book
'11 Configurations' publ. 1945
26.5 × 26 cm
signed lower right

3 Ein Nabel   1923
lithograph, No. 3 from '7 Arpaden Mappe 5'
publ. 1923
45 × 35 cm

4 Personnage Assis   1928
painted board relief mounted on masonite
29.2 × 22.8 cm

5 Form   1934
wood relief
50 × 50 cm

6 Etude Relief   1942
indian ink and collage on paper
42.5 × 37.5 cm
signed on verso

7 Untitled   1947
lithograph
19.5 × 13.8 cm
signed twice

8 Untitled   *c.* 1950
collage
21.5 × 16 cm
signed on verso

Ella Bergmann-Michel

1896 Born in Paderborn, Westphalia. 1915-18 Studied in Weimar. 1918-19 Studio in Weimar. 1919 Married Robert Michel and worked independently in Weimar. 1920 Returned with Robert Michel to his house Schmelzmühle, in Vockenhausen. 1923-25 'Nassauischer Kunstverein' Wiesbaden with El Lissitzky and Kurt Schwitters. 1926 Kunsthalle, Mannheim, 1927 'Werkbund' Mart-Stam-Haus, Stuttgart; travelled in Holland with Kurt Schwitters. 1928 Member of Societé Anonyme, U.S.A.; travelling exhibitions U.S.A. 1929 'Abstract and Surrealist Painting and Sculpture' Frankfurt and Zurich. 1930 Documentary Shorts; collaboration. 'The New Frankfurt' Section Film. 1932 'Abstrakte Kunst' Frankfurt. 1933-45 No artistic work, mainly agricultural work. 1937-39 Studio in London. 1960-62 Lords Gallery, London; 1963 'Pioniere der Bildcollage' Schloss Morsbroich, Leverkusen; 'Shrift en Beeld' Holland. 1964 'Cinquante ans de Collage' Musée St. Etienne and Paris. 1964-65 'Was da ist' Galerie Loehr, Frankfurt-Niederursel. 1967 Gulbenkian Gallery, Newcastle; 'Collage '67' Städische Galerie im Lenbachhaus, Munich. 1968 'Collage zur Assemblage' Institute of Modern Art, Nürnberg; '50 Year Retrospective' Gallery Waddell, New York; 'Collagen aus sechs Jahrzehnten' Kunstverein, Frankfurt and Kunstgewerbemuseum, Zurich. 1969 Queen's Gallery, Belfast; 'Industrie und Technik' Wilhelm-Lehmbruck-Museum, Duisburg and Poland. 1970 'Ella Bergmann-Michel & Robert Michel; Collagen' Kunstverein, Paderborn; 'The Non-Objective World 1914-24' Annely Juda Fine Art, London. 1971 'The Non-Objective World 1924-39' Annely Juda Fine Art, London; Galerie Jean Chauvelin, Paris: Galleria Milano, Milan. 'Deutsche Avantgarde' Galerie Gmurzynska-Bargera, Cologne. Died at Vockenhausen on 8th August.

9   Mit drei weissen Pfeilen (B 180)   1924
    (Herta Wescher Spektrum)
    indian ink and collage on paper
    75 × 60 cm
    signed, dated and numbered lower centre

10 Rotationsprozesse (B 190)   1925
    indian ink and collage on paper
    74.5 × 62 cm
    signed, dated and numbered lower right

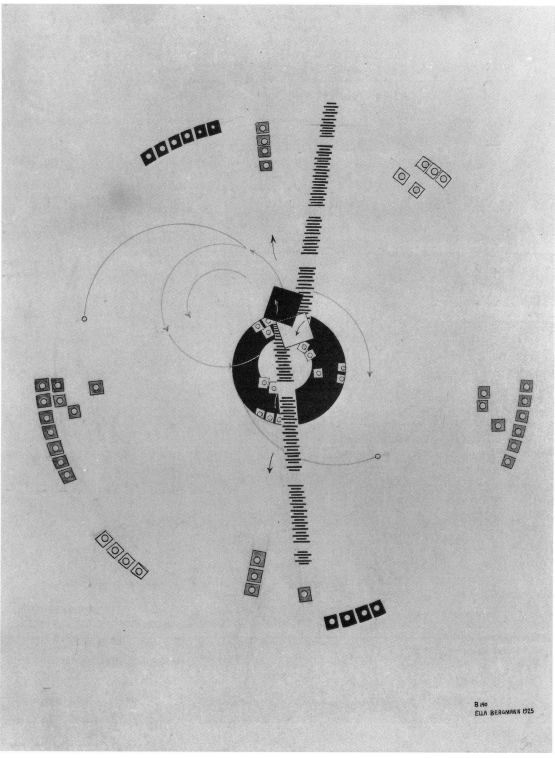

Max Bill

Born 1908 in Winterthur. Active as architect, painter, sculptor, writer. After studying at School of Applied Art, Zurich, taught architecture at Bauhaus from 1927 to 1929. 1928 Took part in 'Young painters of the Bauhaus' exhibition Dessau. Settled in Zurich 1929. 1930 Visited Paris and Italy. 1931 First glass picture. 1932 Joined the group 'Abstraction-Création' together with Hans Arp. 1933 Met Vantongerloo. Moved into the house which he designed himself. 1935 Salon de l'Art mural. 1936 Exhibited in the Swiss Pavilion at the Triennale of Milan where he was awarded first prize. 1937 Alliance, international artists association, London. Exhibition 'Abstract Art' at the Stedelijk Museum, Amsterdam. 1944 'Concrete Art', Basle Kunsthalle. 1944-1945 Appointed teacher at the Zurich School of Applied Art. Beginning of activities in industrial aesthetics. 1951 Plans for the Swiss Pavilion at the Milan Triennale. 1951-1958 Director of the Hochschule für Gestaltung in Ulm. 1957 Studio Zurich. 1964 Chief architect of 'Form and Presentation' Swiss National Exhibition Lausanne. 1967 Professor at the Academy Hamburg. 1968 Awarded the Art Prize of the city of Zurich. 1968-1969 One man shows in major German museums. 1969 Biennale Nuremberg. 1970 Venice Biennale. 1970-1974 Numerous one-man shows. 1974-1975 Travelling exhibition Albright-Knox Gallery, Buffalo, Los Angeles County Museum and San Francisco Museum of Art. Numerous museum and one-man shows since. Lives and works in Zurich.

11 Entsprechungen 1965
oil on canvas
31 × 61 cm

Alexander Calder

1898 Born in Philadelphia, U.S.A. 1915-18 Studied mechanical engineering at the Stevens Institute of Technology, Hoboken, New Jersey. 1919-23 Worked as a draughtsman and engineer in West Coast Logging, New York. 1923 Joined the Art Student' League with George Lucks, Guy de Bois, Beardman Robinson and John Sloan. 1925-26 Worked as an illustrator on the National Police Gazette. 1926-27 Joined the Academie de la Grande Chaumiere, Paris. Started working on wood sculptures and the manufacture of miniature circuses. 1930 First met and was influenced by Piet Mondrian. Started making his first experimental abstract works, at the same time he became a member of the Abstraction-Création Group. 1931 His first mobiles appeared in Paris. 1933 Moved back to Connecticut. 1935 Married Louisa James. 1939 1st Prize Plexiglass Sculpture Competition, Museum of Modern Art, New York. 1952 1st Prize for Sculpture, 36th Biennale di Venezia. 1958 1st Prize Carnegie International, Pittsburgh. 1960 Gold Medal, Architectural League, New York. 1962 Creative Arts Award, Brandeis University, Waltham, Massachusetts. 1971 Gold Medal, National Institute of Arts and Letters, Washington DC. 1976 Died in New York City.

12 Mobile with Numbered Elements *c.* 1932
aluminium and wire
approx: 63.5 × 107 cm
each element numbered 1-13

13 The 'T' Tree 1940
painted metal stabile
148 × 67.5 × 72.5 cm

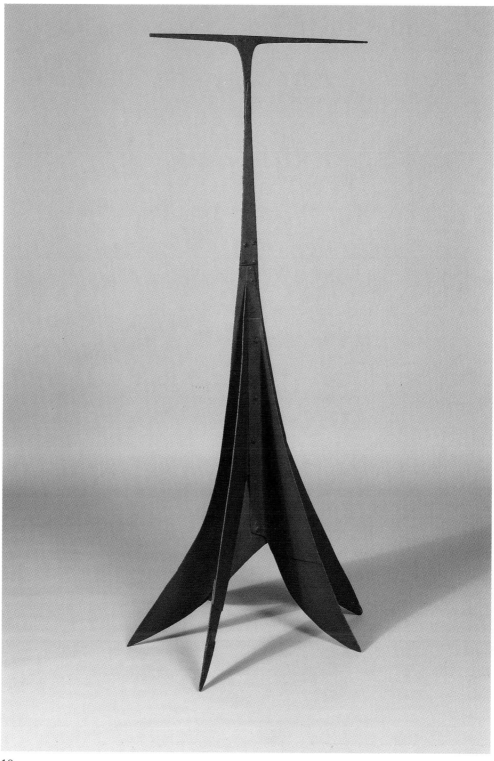

Ilya Chashnik

Born 1902 in Lithuania. From 1903 on he lived in Vitebsk, where he later attended the Vitebsk Art Practical-Institute. There he later studied under Malevich. 1919 Onwards was co-founder of Posnovis (Posledovateli novogo iskusstva – Followers of the New Art) later called Unovis (Utverditeli novogo iskusstva – Affirmers of the New Art) in Vitebsk; within the group, led by Malevich, worked closely with Vera Ermolaeva, Lazar Khidekel, Gustav Klucis, El Lissitzky, Suetin and Lev Yudin; with Khidekel edited the group's journal *AERO*. 1922 With Malevich, Suetin, Yudin and others moved to the Petrograd Inkhuk where he assisted Malevich with the architectural constructions, *'arkhitektony'* and *'planity'*, and worked on ceramic designs at the Lomonosov factory as well as on his own Suprematist easel paintings and textile designs. With Nikolai Suetin he was one of Malevich's closest collaborators. Died 1929 in Leningrad. 1978 Ilja G. Tschaschnik (1902 Ljucite–1929 Leningrad) Kunstmuseum, Dusseldorf; Bauhaus-Archiv Museum für Gestaltung, Berlin.

14 Cup and Saucer
porcelain
height: 7.7 cm
diameter: 14.6 cm

Vassily Ermilov

Born in Kharkov in 1884, Vassil Dimitrievich Ermilov attended the school of decorative arts from 1905-1909, followed by a period of study in the school of painting (1910-1911) under Steinberg, Grot and Zagonov. 1913 he worked in the studio of the 'fauve' painter Ilija Mashkov in Moscow. 1914 His name appeared in public discussions with Marinetti and from that same year date his first Cubo-futurist compositions. The war interrupted his artistic work. Back in Kharkov in 1917, he began exhibiting Suprematist work in 1919. 1918-1922 He was in charge of the Studio of the Decoration of the City, and it was Ermilov who produced the most famous posters for the ROSTA, as well as the propaganda train, *Red Ukraine* in 1921. From 1922, he taught at the Technikum of Art in Kharkov, and at the same time began his Constructivist inspired work, experimenting with the different textures of wood and metal. He gave great prominence to typography, constructions for urban use (public platforms, kiosks) and the theatre, for which his sets for Keiser's *Gaz* (Theatre of the Proletkult in Kharkov, 1922) remains famous. For his remarkable typographical work he was invited to participate in the 'Pressa' in Cologne (1928) where he presented the propaganda panel *Generator* which was designed with an original lettering called *Ermilov*. 1927 His panels and collapsible propaganda stands (with prefabricated elements planned for serial production) were shown in Kharkov at the exhibition '10 Years of Soviet Power' where they drew considerable attention and were later reproduced. At the end of his life he was able to see his retrospective exhibition, held in Kharkov in 1963. Died 1968.

15 Colour System Composition   *c.* 1923
collage on card
28.4 × 40 cm

Alexandra Exter

Born 1882 in Belestok near Kiev. Until 1907 attended the Kiev Art School. 1907 Exhibited for the first time with the group 'La Rose bleue' in Moscow. 1908 Onwards was a regular visitor to Paris and other Western European cities; took part in several Kiev exhibitions including David Burliuk's 'The Link' and that of the journal 'Mir Iskusstva' (World of Art). Represented at the St. Petersburg 'New Society of Artists' 1908, 1909 and the 'Moscow Salon' 1911-1912. 1912 Moved to St. Petersburg. 1915-1916 Contributed to 'Tramway V' and 'The Shop' and began her professional theatre work for Innokentii Annensky's 'Thamira Khytharedes' produced by Aleksander Tairov at his Chamber Theatre, Moscow—the first of several collaborations with Tairov. 1918 Founded her own studio in Kiev where she created huge Suprematist designs for several agit-steamers on the Dnepr River with her pupils. 1921 Contributed to '5 x 5=25' organised by Rodchenko. Turned to textile design while still maintaining her interest in stage design. 1923 Began work on her sets and costumes for the film 'Aelita' (produced 1924); designed decorations for the First Agricultural and Handicraft-Industrial Exhibition in Moscow. 1924 Emigrated and settled in Paris. Studied stage and costume design at the Modern Art Academy, Paris. 1927 Exhibited at the gallery 'Der Sturm' Berlin. Died 1949 at Fontenay-aux-roses.

16 Composition Dynamique *c.* 1916
gouache on paper
65 × 51 cm
studio stamp on verso

Sam Francis

1923 Born in San Mateo, California. 1941-53 Studied medical sciences University of California, Berkeley. 1948-50 B.A. and M.A. in Art. 1950 Academie Fernand Leger, Paris. 1943-45 Served in U.S. Army Air Corps. 1944 Spinal tuberculosis diagnosed. Began painting in hospitals, Denver and San Francisco. Studied privately with David Park. 1947 Convalescence in Artists' Colony, Carmel, California. 1950-52 Travelled in France. Summers in Aix-en-Provence. 1954 In California. 1956-58 Travelled extensively, visiting New York, Mexico, Japan, Thailand, India, Italy. 1959 Further illness, California. 1961 Berne, Switzerland. 1968 Collaborated with group *Single Wing Turquoise Bird*. Awards: 1962 International Biennial Exhibition of Prints, Tokyo. 1963 Dunn International Prize, Tate Gallery, London, and Tamarind Fellowship. 1969 Hon. Doctorate, University of California, Berkeley. Individual shows: 1963 Kestner-Gellschaft, Hanover. 1964 Pasadena Art Museum, California. 1965 Wurtembergischer Kunstverein, Stuttgart. 1966 Pasadena Art Museum, California. 1967 Museum of Fine Arts, Houston, Texas. University Art Museum, Berkeley, California. 1968 Kunsthalle, Basle; Badischer Kunstverein, Karlsruhe, Germany; Stedelijk Museum, Amsterdam; Centre National d'Art Contemporain, Paris. 1970 Los Angeles County Museum of Art. 1971 André Emmerich Gallery, New York. 1972 Albright-Knox Art Gallery, Buffalo, New York. Lives and works in California.

17 Untitled 1955
watercolour
44.4 × 35.5 cm

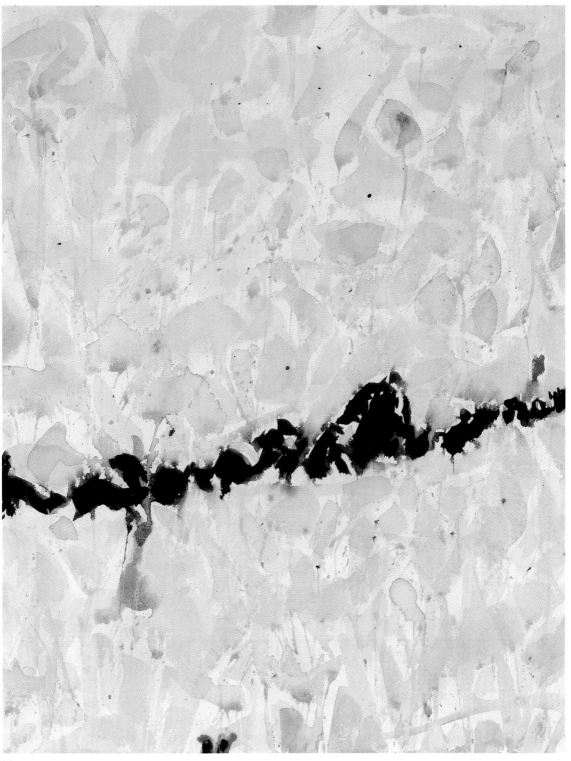

Otto Freundlich

Born 1878 in Stolp (Pomerania). 1909 Settled in Paris and lived in the 'Bateau-Lavoir' with Picasso and Herbin as neighbours. Beginning of his first sculptures as well as his paintings. 1910 Exhibited in Paris. 1911 In Amsterdam and 1912 in Cologne. 1919 Made his first non-figurative compositions. 1924 Returned to Paris. Participated at Salon des Indépendants and Surin-dépendents exhibitions. 1930 Joined the group 'Cercle et Carré'. 1931 Joined the group 'Abstraction-Création'. 1934 Exhibited with Erni at Abstraction-Création. 1936 Opened a private Academy under the name 'Le Mur'. 1937 Some of his works in the exhibition 'Entartete Kunst' Munich. 14 works were removed from German museums. 1938 Retrospective at the Galeria Jeanne Bucher, Paris. Also had a one-man show at the Galerie Bucher-Myrbor, Paris and had works in 'Abstracte Art' Stedelijk Museum, Amsterdam and 'Modern German Art' New Burlington Gallery, London. 1939 Participated in various gallery shows in Paris. Was interned. 1940 Liberated with the help of Picasso. 1942 In St. Martin-de-Fenouillet. 1943 Deported and probably died in a concentration camp.

18 Abstract Composition   *c.* 1939
    pastel on paper
    48.5 × 42 cm
    initialled lower right 'F'

19 Preparatory Sketch for
    'Abstract Composition'   *c.* 1939
    pencil on buff paper
    24.7 × 21.6 cm

Naum Gabo

Born 1890 in Briansk (Russia). 1915 Made first constructions using the name Gabo. 1917 Returned to Russia. 1920 First public exhibition in the open air on Tverskoi Boulevard, Moscow. Wrote the 'Realistic Manifesto' published in Moscow with his brother Antoine. First constructions with motor. 1922 Left Moscow for Berlin. Exhibited in the 'Erste Russische Kunstaustellung' at the Galerie van Diemen, Berlin. 'Project for a Monument for an Observatory'. 1924 Exhibited with Pevsner at Galerie Percier, Paris. 1924-25 'Project for a Monument for an Airport'. 1926 Exhibited for the first time in America at the Little Review Gallery, New York with van Doesburg and Pevsner. Designed set, properties and costumes for Diaghilev's ballet 'La Chatte'. 1930 First one-man exhibition of constructions at the Kestner-Gesellschaft, Hanover. 1931 Project for the Palace of the Soviets, Moscow. 1932 Left Berlin for Paris. 1932-35 Member of the group 'Abstraction-Création'. 1935 First visit to England. 1936 Exhibited in 'Abstract and Concrete' at the Lefèvre Gallery, London; 'Cubism and Abstract Art' at the Museum of Modern Art, New York and exhibited with Pevsner at the Chicago Arts Club. Married Miriam Israels in London. 1937 Edited with J. L. Martin and Ben Nicholson 'Circle'. Works exhibited in 'Konstruktivisten' at Kunsthalle Basle and 'Constructive Art' London Gallery, London. 1938 One-man exhibition at the London Gallery, London. 1939 At the outbreak of war moved to Carbis Bay, Cornwall. 1946 Left England for the United States. 1948 Exhibited with Pevsner at the Museum of Modern Art, New York. 1952 Exhibition with Josef Albers at the Chicago Arts Club. 1953 One-man exhibition at the Pierre Matisse Gallery, New York; with Alexander Calder at the Wadsworth Atheneum, Hartford. 1953-54 Professor at Harvard University Graduate School of Architecture. 1954 Awarded Guggenheim Fellowship. 1955 Commissioned to make sculpture for the Bijenkorf Building, Rotterdam. 1956 Commissioned by Wallace K. Harrison to make bas-relief for the U.S. Rubber Company, Rockefeller Centre, New York, completed in November. 1960 Prize from Brandeis University, Massachusetts. 1962 Visited his three brothers in Moscow and Leningrad. 1965-66 Retrospective exhibition at the Stedlijk Museum, Amsterdam; Kunshalle Mannheim; Wilhelm-Lehmbruck-Museum, Duisburg; Kunsthaus Zurich; Moderna Museet, Stockholm and Tate Gallery, London. 1970 Commissioned to make fountain, installed at St. Thomas's Hospital 1975. 1971 Awarded the Hon. K.B.E. 1970-72 Travelling exhibition Louisiana Museum, Humblebaeck; Nasjonalgalereit, Oslo; Nationalgalerie, Berlin; Kunstverein, Hanover; Musée de Peinture et Sculpture, Grenoble; Musée National d'Art Moderne, Paris; Gulbenkian Foundation, Lisbon. 1973 Commissioned to make sculpture for the Nationalgalerie, Berlin. 1976-77 One-man exhibition at the Tate Gallery, London. 1977 Died in Connecticut.

20 Construction in a Square   1937
perspex, on anodised aluminium base
44.5 × 44.5 × 16 cm
(C.R. 12.2)

21 Study for 'Logan Rock'   1930s
pencil on graph paper
28.2 × 21.8 cm
initialled lower right

22 Two Studies mounted together for a
Construction and Painting   c. 1940s
pencil on paper
30.4 × 32.6 cm

23 Sketch   1940
crayon on paper
31 × 29 cm
signed and dated lower right

24 Sketch for a Vertical Construction   c. 1952
pencil on paper
38 × 27 cm
initialled lower right

25 Construction in Space: Suspended   1957/65
perspex, nylon monofilament, gilded
phosphor-bronze cradle; on aluminium base
51.3 × 61.6 × 52.7 cm
on integral base: 3.2 × 68.5 × 19.1 cm
(C.R. 70.12)

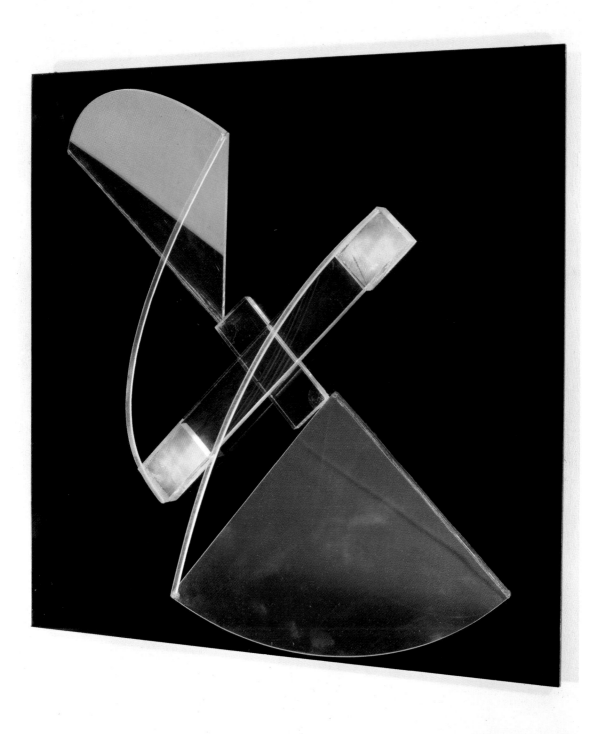

Camille Graeser

Born in Carouge, Geneva, Switzerland 1892. 1913-15
Studied Kunstgewerbeschule Stuttgart. 1915-1916
Contact with Herwarth Walden 'Der Sturm' in Berlin.
1926-27 Participated Weissenhof settlement Stuttgart,
housing project Mies van der Rohe. 1933 Returned to
Switzerland, interested exclusively in constructivist art.
Exhibitions: 1938 Kunsthalle Basle. 1948 and 1950
Réalités Nouvelles, Paris. 1958 Biennale Venice. 1960
'Concrete Art, 50 years development', Zurich. 1961-62
Galerie Denise René 'Art abstrait constructif inter-
national', Paris. 1964 Retrospective Kunsthaus Zurich.
1967 Kunsthalle, Basle. 1968 Gimpel and Hanover,
Zurich. Gimpel Fils, London. 1969 Biennal Sao Paulo,
Biennale Nuremberg. 1970 Gimpel and Weizenhoffer,
New York. Museo de Art Moderna, Rio de Janeiro. 1971
The Swiss Avantgarde, New York. 1972 Gimpel and
Hanover, Zurich. 1972-73 The Non-Objective World
1939-55 Annely Juda Fine Art, London and on to Basle
and Milan. The Museum Tel-Aviv 'Contemporary Swiss
Art'. Died 1980.

26 Realisation mit grauem Quadrat   1960-63
oil on canvas
80 × 40 cm
signed on verso

Al Held

1928 Born in New York. 1948-49 Studied at the Art Students League, New York with Harry Sternberg. 1950-52 Studied at the Grande Chaumière, Paris with Zadkine. Associated with, amongst others, Bill Rivers, Ellsworth Kelly, Sam Francis and Ken Noland. 1953 Returned to New York. 1962-80 Professor at Yale University. His one-man exhibitions include: 1952 Galerie Huit, Paris. 1959, 60, 61 and 62 Poindexter Gallery, New York. 1961 Bonino Gallery, Buenos Aires. 1964 Galerie Renée Ziegler, Zurich. 1965 André Emmerich Gallery, New York and regularly since. 1966 Stedelijk Museum, Amsterdam; Galerie Muller, Stuttgart. 1967 Galerie Renée Ziegler, Zurich. 1968 Institute of Contemporary Art of The University of Pennsylvania, Philadelphia; Contemporary Arts Museum, Houston; San Francisco Museum of Art, San Francisco; Corcoran Gallery of Art, Washington, D.C. 1970 Galerie Renée Ziegler, Zurich. 1971 Donald Morris Gallery, Detroit. 1974 Galerie André Emmerich, Zurich; Donald Morris Gallery, Detroit; Galerie Muller, Cologne; Whitney Museum of American Art, New York. 1975 Adler Castillo Gallery, Caracas. 1977 Galerie André Emmerich, Zurich; Galerie Renée Ziegler, Zurich; Galerie Roger d'Amecourt, Paris; Annely Juda Fine Art, London; Donald Morris Gallery, Birmingham, Michigan. 1978 Institute of Contemporary Art, Boston; Marianne Friedland Gallery, Toronto. 1980 Gimpel-Hanover and André Emmerich Galerien, Zurich; Annely Juda Fine Art, London; Quadrat Bottrop Moderne Galerie, Germany; Robert Miller Gallery, New York. 1981 Gimpel-Hanover and André Emmerich Gallerien, Zurich. 1982 Juda Rowan Gallery, London; Robert Miller Gallery, New York. 1983 Donald Morris Gallery, Birmingham, Michigan. 1984 Gimpel-Hanover and André Emmerich Galerien, Zurich; Richard Gray Gallery, Chicago; Marianne Friedland Gallery, Toronto. 1986 John Berggruen Gallery, San Francisco. 1987 Juda Rowan Gallery, London. He lives and works in New York.

27 Roberta's Trip   1985
acrylic on canvas
244 × 366 cm
signed and dated on verso

Barbara Hepworth

1903 Born in Wakefield, Yorkshire. 1920-21 Studied at Leeds School of Art with Henry Moore and Raymond Coxon. 1921-24 Studied sculpture at the Royal College of Art, London. 1924-26 Travelled and studied in Italy, attending the British School in Rome. 1926 Lived in Hampstead, London until 1939. 1930-36 Member of the Seven and Five Society, London. 1931 Met Ben Nicholson. 1931-32 Associated with Henry Moore and Ivon Hitchens, London. 1932 Travelled in France, meeting Sophie Täuber-Arp and Picasso. Married Ben Nicholson (divorced 1951). 1933 Member of the Abstraction-Création Group, Paris and the Unit One Group, London. 1934 Associated with Naum Gabo, Piet Mondrian and Alexander Calder. 1937 Collaborated with Nicholson and Gabo on the magazine 'Circle', London. 1939 Lived briefly in Carbis Bay, Cornwall before settling in St. Ives. 1948 Co-founder with Naum Gabo, Adrian Stokes, Bernard Leach and others of the Penwith Society of Arts, St. Ives. 1949 Established Trewyn Studio, St. Ives. 1950 Travelled to Venice. 1951-55 Numerous stage designs. 1958 Commander, Order of British Empire, London. 1959 Grand Prize, 5th Sao Paulo Biennale. 1960 Honorary Degree, University of Birmingham, England. 1961 Honorary Degree, University of Leeds, England. 1963 Foreign Minister's Award, Tokyo Biennale. 1965 Created Dame of the British Empire. 1966 Honorary Degree, University of Exeter, England. 1968 Honorary Degree, Oxford University, England and appointed Trustee of the Tate Gallery, London. 1975 Died in St. Ives, Cornwall. The Hepworth Museum established in St. Ives.

28 Discs in Echelon   1935
polished bronze, edition of 4
length: 52.7 cm

29 Disc with Strings (Sun)   1969
polished bronze with string
50.8 × 47 × 10.2 cm

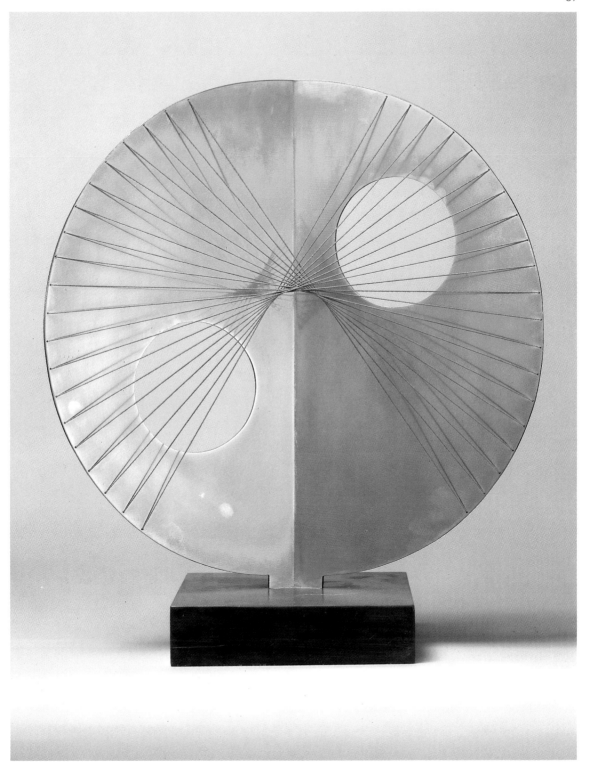

Hans Hinterreiter

Born Winterthur 1902. Studied architecture at the Technical College. Knew Max Bill also born in Winterthur. Met Bill in 1938 again and discovered a new kind of painting. Developed Wilhelm Oswald's colour theory and initial design for a 'form' theory and produced a composition scheme for form and colour. 1942 First exhibition with 'Allianz' at the Kunsthaus, Zürich. A Spanish group 'Equipo 7' took over some of Hinterreiter's methods. 1971 Exhibition of small works 1930-40 Neue Galerie, Baden-Baden. 1973 Retrospective Kunstmuseum, Winterthur. 1977 A travelling exhibition throughout Europe on the occasion of his 75th birthday. Lives and works in Ibiza.

30 Opus 86   1959
egg tempera on hardboard
63 × 72.6 cm
signed, titled and dated on verso

Hannah Hoch

Born 1st November, 1889 at Gotha, Thuringia. 1912 Began her studies at the School of Decorative Art in Berlin with Harold Bengen. 1915 Continued her studies with Emil Orlik. First met Raoul Hausmann. 1916 First abstract painting. 1918 On holiday at the island of Usedom, on the Baltic with Hausmann. First photomontage. Dada dolls. 1919 Participated in the first Dada exhibition at the Graphischen Kabinett J. B. Neuman, Berlin. Member of November Group. 1920 Participated in the First Grand Dada Exhibition at Dr. Otto Burchard's Gallery, Lutzowufer 13, Berlin with collages, reliefs and dolls. Visited Rome. 1921 February 10 with Hausmann and Mynona staged a lecture evening in the Berliner Sezession. September with Hausmann and Schwitters organised a Dada Tournée in Prague entitled 'Anti-Dada-Merz'. 1922 First grotto in Schwitters Merzbau in Hanover. Met Theo van Doesburg. 1923 Hans Arp worked in her atelier in Berlin. Beginning of the 'Portrait' series of collages. 1924 First visit to Paris. Met Mondrian. Designs for an Anti-Revue – costumes and set with Schwitters and H. Stuckenschmidt. 1925 Second grotto in Schwitters Merzbau, Hanover. Beginning of the series of photomontages: 'In an ethnographic museum'. Second visit to Paris. Painted 'Roma'. 1926-1929 Lived in Holland. 1929 Participated in the Werkbund Exhibition 'Film and Photo'. 1934 Exhibition of 42 Collages at Brnö, Czechoslovakia. 1939 Moved to Heiligensee North Berlin. 1965 Elected to Berlin Akademie der Künste. 1974 Exhibition at the National Museum of Modern Art, Kyoto. 1976-1977 Exhibition at the Nationalgalerie, Berlin. 1978 Died in Berlin.

31 Konstruktion mit Blau   1919
watercolour
30.5 × 24.4 cm
signed and dated lower right

32 Gelbe Bahn   1919
watercolour
45 × 47 cm
initialled, titled and dated

H. Höch, 19

KUNSTSCHAU AUF ????

Gottfried Honegger

Born 1917 in Zurich where he studied art. 1939 Went to Paris to paint. Returned to Switzerland at outbreak of War. First one-man exhibition at Chichio Haller, Zurich, 1950. Travelled extensively and lived in New York from 1958 to 1960 when he first showed at the Martha Jackson Gallery and again in 1964. Since 1963 regular one-man exhibitions at Gimpel & Hanover Galerie, Zurich and at Gimpel Fils, London in 1964 and 1968. First showed at Annely Juda Fine Art in 1979 and at the Juda Rowan Gallery in 1983. Amongst his other important one-man exhibitions are those at the Württembergischer Kunstverein, Stuttgart 1966; Kunsthaus, Zurich 1967; Museum am Ostwall, Dortmund 1968; Valley House Gallery, Dallas 1969 and 1972; Galerie Swart, Amsterdam 1972; Badischer Kunstverein, Karlsruhe 1972; Galerie Teufel, Cologne 1972; Galerie d'Art Moderne, Basle 1974; Galerie Denise René, Paris 1974 and 1975; XIII Bienal de Sao Paulo, Brazil 1975; Musée d'Art Moderne de la Ville de Paris 1978; Galerie Nouvelles Images, The Hague 1978 and 1983; Ulmer Museum, Ulm 1981; Galerie Müller-Roth, Stuttgart 1983; Kunsthaus Zug, Zug 1984; Galerie Brownstone+Cie, Paris 1988. He is represented in numerous public collections, Centre National d'Art Contemporain, Paris; Israel Museum, Jerusalem; Carnegie Institute, Pittsburgh; Dallas Museum of Fine Arts, Texas; Hirshhorn Museum, Washington D.C.; Museum of Modern Art, New York; Louisiana Museum, Humlebaek; Musée National d'Art Moderne, Centre Georges Pompidou, Paris; Staatsgalerie Stuttgart; Albright-Knox Art Gallery, Buffalo. Monograph on his paintings and sculpture by Serge Lemoine, published by Waser, Zurich 1984. Since 1961 he lives and works in Paris and Zurich.

33 Z 924   1986
acrylic on canvas
182 × 60 cm

34 Monoform 19   1987
marble
height: 80 cm

Malcolm Hughes

Born in Manchester in 1920. Studied at Manchester and Royal College of Art. Taught at Bath Academy of Art, Corsham, Chelsea and Slade School of Art. 1969 Cofounded the Systems Group. 1982 Emeritus Reader in Fine Art, University of London; Honorary Research Fellow, University College, London. 1984 Honorary Fellow, University College of Wales. First one-man exhibition was at the I.C.A. Gallery in 1965. 1967 Axiom Gallery; 1972 Lucy Milton Gallery; 1983 Juda Rowan Gallery; 1985 'Working Drawings', University Gallery, Leeds. Amongst the group exhibitions that have included his work are 1967 'Constructions', Arts Council U.K. touring exhibition; 'Four Artists: Reliefs, Constructions and Drawings', Victoria and Albert Museum, 1971; 'Systems', Whitechapel Art Gallery and U.K. tour 1972; 'Art as Thought Process', Serpentine Gallery, 1974; 'New Work 2', Hayward Gallery, London 1975; 'Arte Inglese Oggi', Milan 1976; 'British Artists of the Sixties', Tate Gallery and Annely Juda Fine Art (with Dilworth, Lowe and Steele) 1977; 'Constructive Context', Warehouse Gallery and U.K. tour, 1978; '8 +8', Annely Juda Fine Art, 1980; 1983 'Concepts in Construction', selected by Irving Sandler and touring U.S.A. 1983 'Nature-Structure-Construction' Arbeitskreis Kemin Taidemuseo, Finland. 1984 'Constructive Tendencies in Europe', Galerie Konstructiv Tendens, Stockholm, Sweden. Participation in 'Exhibiting Space', London. Lives and works in London.

35 A work in 2 Parts   1987
maquette, oil on hardboard, in 2 parts
28 × 28 cm; 39.5 × 39.5 cm

Ivan Kliun

Born 1873 in Kiev. Studied art in Warsaw and Kiev. During the early 1900s attended private studios in Moscow including those of Fedor Rerberg and Ilya Mashkov. 1907 Met Malevich. 1910 co-founded the Moscow Salon. 1913 In close contact with Malevich, Matiushin and Kruchenykh. 1913-1914 Contributed to the last 'Soiuz molodezhi' (Union of Youth) exhibition, St. Petersburg. 1915 Illustrated Kruchenykh's 'Tainye poroki akademikov' (Secret Vices of Academicians). Participated in 'Tramway V: First Futurist Exhibition of Paintings', Petrograd. 1915-1916 Took part in 'The Last Futurist Exhibition of Pictures: 0.10', Petrograd; 'Magazin' (The Store) and 'Bubnovyi valet' (Jack of Diamonds), Moscow. 1917 Named director of the Central Exhibition Bureau of Narkompros. 1918-1921 Professor of painting at Svomas and later at Vkhutemas. 1919 Took part in the Fifth and Tenth State Exhibitions, Moscow. 1922 Sent work to the 'First Russian Art Exhibition' Galerie van Diemen, Berlin. 1923 Designed a series of Futurist publications including Kruchenykh's 'Faktura slova' (Verbal Texture). 1925 Member of the Four Arts group. 1942 Died in Moscow.

36 Untitled   1916
   wood relief
   37.5 × 17.5 × 7 cm
   signed and dated top left

37 4 Compositions   c. 1916-22
   watercolour and pencil on paper
   each approx: 7 × 7 cm

38 2 Compositions   c.1916-22
   watercolour and pencil on paper
   each 5.2 × 8.2 cm

39 Suprematist Composition   c. 1918
   crayon on paper
   14.5 × 9.5 cm

40 Composition   1920
   oil on paper laid down on board
   21 × 31.7 cm
   signed and dated lower right

Gustav Klucis

Born 1895 near Riga (Latvia). Arrived 1918 in Moscow with a group of Latvians who were to be the personal bodyguard of Lenin at the Kremlin. 1918 Became a student at Wchutemas and worked in the studio of Pevsner who influenced him during that period. 1919 Abstract painting and non-objective constructions (Coll. Tretjekov Gallery, Moscow 'Aksinometric Painting' 1920). 1921 Non-objective constructions with free-standing elements. Friend of El Lissitzky and Tatlin. First photomontage in Russia 1919 with the 'Ville dynamique' as basic composition. During the Twenties Klucis was one of the most important photomontage artists in Russia. According to A. B. Nakov he was one of the most creative and individualistic artists among the Constructivists. He participated in the first photo-montage exhibition in Berlin organised by Domela in 1922 and he constructed a number of propaganda kiosks. During the 20s and 30s he participated in many international exhibitions also in Paris 1925 and 1937. From 1924 onwards he worked at Wchutemas and developed his own colour theory. He disappeared in 1938.

41 Colour Study *c.* 1920
pencil, watercolour and ink on paper
27 × 35 cm
inscribed top right

42 Colour Study *c.* 1920
pencil and watercolour on paper
25 × 37.7 cm
signed on verso, inscribed (rubbed out) lower right

43 Colour Study *c.* 1920
ink and watercolour on paper
26.7 × 20.9 cm
inscribed on verso

44 Architectural Study *c.* 1920/25
gouache, indian ink and pencil on paper laid down on board
39.5 × 24.8 cm

Frantisek Kupka

Born 1871 in Opocno (Bohemia). 1887-1891 Studied at the Academies in Prague and Vienna. 1895 Moved to Paris. Illustrations for magazines. 1911 Changed to rhythmic painting, 'Orphism'. 1914-1918 In the Czech Exile Army in France. 1918 Professor at the Academy, Prague. Published 'La Création dans l'Art plastique', Prague. Several journeys to Prague. 1931 On committee of the group 'Abstraction-Création'. 1936 Took part in the exhibition 'Cubism and Abstract Art' at the Museum of Modern Art in New York. War years spent in Beaugency. 1944 Returned to Puteaux. 1946 Large retrospective at the Galerie S.V.U. Manès in Prague. The State of Czechoslovakia bought about 40 paintings in order to establish a Kupka museum. 1957 Died in Puteaux. 1958 Retrospective at the Musée National d'Art Moderne in Paris. 1963 Eugene Kupka donation to the Musée National d'Art Moderne.

45 Composition 1920-25
gouache
28.1 × 19.2 cm
signed lower left

Henri Laurens

Born 1885 in Paris. Apprenticeship with a sculptor-designer. 1911 Met Braque. 1914-1915 Adopted the cubist aesthetics. Made collages and constructions with steel, wood, plaster and carton. From 1919 created 'bas-reliefs' and 'rondes-bosses'. 1924 Carried out stage designs for the 'Train Bleu' for Diaghilev. By 1927 new directions, returned to volume, massive forms. 1937 Made monumental figures for the 'Pavillon de Sevres' at the International Exhibition of Paris and for the Palais de la Decouverte. Died 1954 in Paris.

46 Guitare   1926
bronze bas-relief, ed. no. 3/6
152 × 91 × 2 cm
initialled and numbered lower right

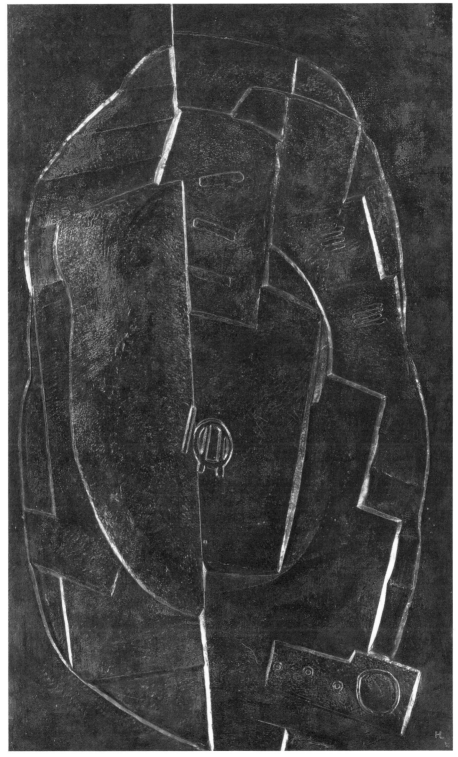

Bart van der Leck

Born in Utrecht 1876. Studied at the State School for Decorative Arts and at the Academy in Amsterdam. 1905 Illustrations for the Song of Songs. 1910 First realistic studies. 1911 Interest in the accentuation of the plane. 1914 Stained glass window 'Mining Industry'. 1916 His stylisation reached a culminating point in 'The Tempest' and 'Harbour-works'. 1917 Abstract compostions, projects for an interior. Joined the De Stijl. 1918 First figurative compositions using elementary symbols. 1919 Made studies in textile techniques. 1928 Designed textiles. 1934 First attempts in interior decoration by distribution of colours. 1935 Made his first studies in ceramics. 1940-1941 Did book illustrations. 1949 and 1952 Designs and execution in colour of interiors in Amsterdam. 1958 Died in Amsterdam.

47 Horse and Foal 1928
watercolour on paper
34 × 47 cm
signed and dated on card on verso

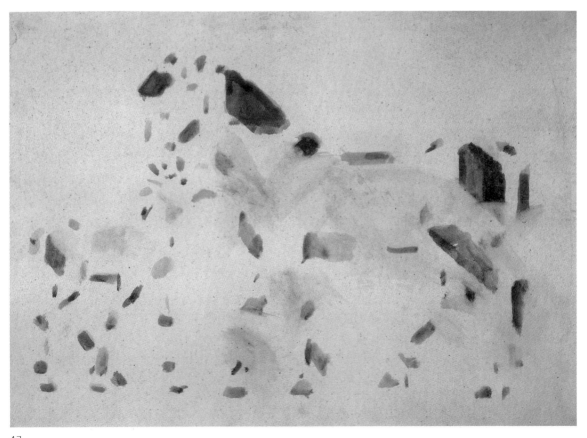

Fernand Leger

1881 Born in Argentan, France. 1897-99 Studied architecture in Caen. 1900-02 Draughtsman for an architect in Paris. 1903 Studied at the 'Ecole des Arts Decoratifs'. 1905-07 Shared a studio with Andre Mare, Paris. 1908-09 Associated with Archipenko, Jacob, Apollinaire, Reverdy, Cendrars, Robert Delaunay and Rousseau in Paris. 1910-12 Attended gatherings at Villon's house in Paris with Gleizes, Le Fauconnier and Kupka amongst others. Later involved with the Section d'Or Group. 1913 First contact with D. H. Kahnweiler. 1920 Met Le Corbusier. 1922 Stage designs for 'La Création du Monde' ballet of Ralf de Mare. 1924 'Le ballet mécanique' first film with his own scenario. 1925 Collaborated with Robert Delaunay on an exhibition at the Arts Décoratifs, Paris. 1928 Travelled to Berlin. 1931 First trip to the U.S.A. 1932 Started teaching at La Grande Chaumière', Paris. 1935 First exhibition at the Museum of Modern Art, New York and at the Art Institute in Chicago. 1937 Murals 'Le transport des forces' for the Palais de la Découverte, Paris. 1940-45 Fled to New York. Taught at Yale University, New Haven, Connecticut and Mills College, Oakland, California. 1945 Returned to France. 1946 Mosaic for the Church at Assy, France. 1955 First Prize at the third Sao Paulo Biennale. Died in Gif-sur-Yvette, France.

48 Compositon sur Fond Rouge   1945
oil on canvas
92.4 × 73 cm
signed and dated lower right; signed, titled and dated on verso

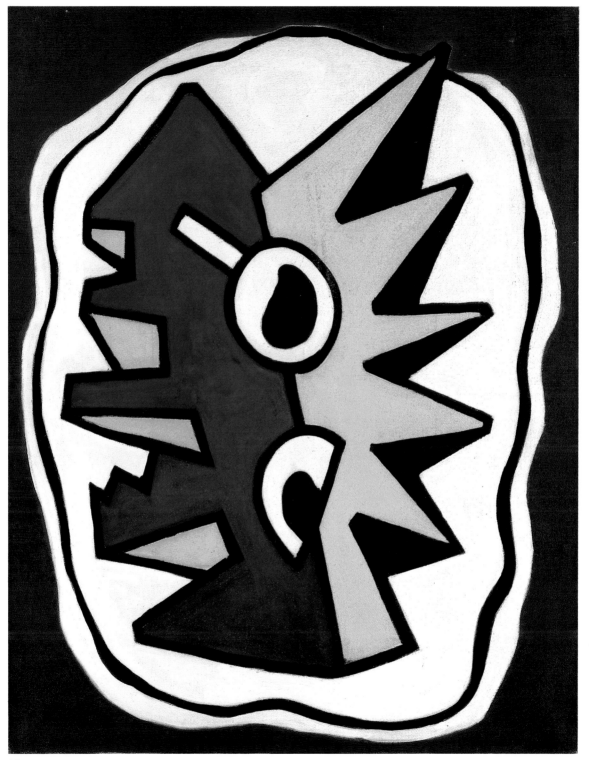

Lazar El Lissitzky

Born 1890 in Polschinok near Smolensk. Studied in Smolensk. 1909-1914 Studied Technical College, Darmstadt. 1914 Returned to Moscow. Took part in exhibitions. Illustrations for children's books. After the Revolution posts in art organisations in Moscow. 1919 Professorship in Vitebsk. Meeting with Malevich. Turned to non-objective art. Formed his first 'PROUN' picture constructions. Participation between 1920 and 1922 in the Constructivist movement. 1921 Showed in the 'First Constructivist Exhibition' in Moscow and 1922 in the 'Erste Russische Kunstausstellung', Berlin. 1922 In Berlin, contact with the German avantgarde and the Bauhaus in Weimar. Participated in the Dadaist and Constructivist Congress in Weimar. 1923 Publication of Majakowsky's book 'For Reading Out Loud' with new typography. Friendship with Kurt Schwitters and Theo van Doesburg in Hanover. Advertising for Pelican. Worked on several publications. Due to tuberculosis settled in Switzerland. 1925 Returned to Moscow. Professor at WKHUTEMAS. 1926 Designed an entire room at the 'International Art Exhibition' Dresden and 1927 design of the 'Cabinet of the Abstracts' in the Landesmuseum, Hanover. 1928 Design for the Soviet Pavilion, PRESSA, Cologne. Returned to Moscow, married Sophie Küppers. Exhibition design and graphic work followed collaboration on publications. Died 1941 in Moscow.

49 Untitled   c. 1920s
tempera on canvas
73.5 × 51.5 cm

50 Design for Book Cover   1921
pen, ink and pencil on paper
23 × 15.5 cm
inscribed upper left

"НИСПРОВЕРЖЕНИЕ СТАРОГО МИРА ИСКУССТВ" ДА БУДЕТ
ВЫЧЕРЧЕНО НА ВАШИХ ЛАДОНЯХ."

эл лисицкий

КУС СТ

ИС ВА.

ПРЕОДОЛЕНИЕ

ИНХУК.

Richard Lohse

Born in Zurich 1902. Studied Kunstgewerbeschule, Zurich, 1920-24. Early contact with Klee, Moholy-Nagy, Hans Richter, Täuber-Arp. Evolved through Cubism to vertical-horizontal non-objective designs. Organised Swiss section 'Réalités Nouvelles' Paris 1950. Contact with Pevsner, Vantongerloo, Herbin, Le Corbusier. Exhibited: Galerie Denise René Paris 1948. Réalités Nouvelles 1948, 1950. Milan Triennale 1957. Gallery Chalette 1960. Kunsthaus, Zurich, 1962. 'Art Abstrait Constructif International' Galerie Denise René, Paris 1961. Sao Paulo Biennial 1951. Venice Biennale 1958. Guggenheim International Prize 1958. Venice Biennale 1972. Kunsthalle Basle 1975. Kunsthaus Zurich und Neue Galerie Bottrop 1976. Van Abbemuseum, Eindhoven 1978-1979. Amos Andersen Museum, Helsinki, 1980. Haags Gemeentemuseum, The Hague, Holland and Jan van Eyk Academy, Maastricht, Holland 1983. Free University, Amsterdam 1984. Kunst Museum, Lucerne and Kunstverein Braunschweig, Germany 1985. Vienna Secession 1986. Lives and works in Zurich.

51 Progression von 4 gleichen Gruppen von 1-7   1952-66
oil on canvas
64 × 64 cm

Kasimir Malevich

Born 1879 near Kiev (Ukraine). 1895 Studied at the Art School in Kiev. 1900 Moved to Moscow, continued studies. Contact with the artists of the 'Left Art'. Exhibitions with the avantgarde groups. 1913 Contact with the Futurists. Designs for the opera 'Victory over the Sun' by Kruchenykh. 1914 Met Marinetti. 1914 'Knave of Diamonds' Moscow; 'Salon des Indépendents' Paris. 1915 'Tramway V' and '0.10'. Petrograd; published 'From Cubism to Suprematism'. 1917 'Knave of Diamonds' Moscow. 1919 Succeeded Chagall at the Art School of Vitebsk which was re-named 'Unovis' and had links with Moscow, Smolensk and Saratov. 1920 Published 'Suprematism, 34 Drawings' in Vitebsk. 1922 'Union of New Artistic Currents' Petrograd; 'Erste Russische Kunstaustellung' Galerie van Diemen, Berlin; became director of Inkhuk, Leningrad. 1924 '14th International Art Exhibition' Venice. 1927 Returned to Poland; had a room at the 'Grosse Berliner Kunstaustellung'. 1929 Retrospective at the Tretiakov Gallery, Moscow; Inkhuk closed. 1930 'Russian Contemporary Art' Vienna; 'Soviet Art' Moscow. 1935 'The First Exhibition of Painters from Leningrad' (this was the first official exhibition to be put on after the Communist Decree); died of cancer in Leningrad.

52 Suprematist Composition *c.* 1916
pencil on paper
18.2 × 11 cm

53 Suprematist Composition *c.* 1916
pencil on paper
17 × 11.7 cm

54 Suprematist Composition *c.* 1916
pencil on paper
20.7 × 11.7 cm

55 Suprematist Composition *c.* 1916
pencil on paper
21.5 × 15.2 cm

Kenneth Martin

1903 Born in Sheffield. 1921-23 Studied at Sheffield School of Art. 1923-29 Worked in Sheffield as a designer. 1929-32 Studied at the Royal College of Art, London. 1930 Married Mary Balmford. 1946-47 Visiting Teacher Goldsmiths' College of Art. 1948-49 First Abstract Paintings. 1951 First Kinetic Constructions. 1965 Gold Medal, President of the Italian Council of Ministers, on the occasion of the International Congress of Artists and Critics at Verucchio. 1969 First Chance and Order works. 1969 Death of Mary Martin. 1971 Awarded the OBE. 1976 Honorary Doctorate, Royal College of Art. 1976 Midsummer Prize, City of London. His one-man exhibitions include: 1954 Heffer Gallery, Cambridge (with Mary Martin). 1960 'Essays in Movements', ICA, London (with Mary Martin). 1962 Lords Gallery, London. 1967 Axiom Gallery, London. 1970-71 Arts Council of Great Britain touring exhibition (with Mary Martin). 1970 Waddington Galleries Ltd, London. 1974 Waddington Galleries Ltd, London; Galerie Swart, Amsterdam. 1975 Tate Gallery Retrospective, London; Galerie m, Bochum. 1976 Galerie m, Den Haag and Dusseldorf; 'The Sculptor at Work' (with Henry Moore) Scottish National Gallery of Modern Art, Edinburgh. 1977 Arts Council 'Working Methods' touring Exhibition; 'Kenneth Martin: Drawings and Prints', Museum of Modern Art, Oxford. 1978 Waddington and Tooth Galleries, London; Galerie Lydia Megert, Bern, Switzerland. 1979 Galerie Swart, Amsterdam. Yale Center for British Art, New Haven, Connecticut (retrospective exhibition). 1980 Galerie Giles Gheerbrant, Montreal (drawings); Galerie m, Bochum; Sperone Westwater Fischer, New York. 1981 Waddington Galleries Ltd, London; Galerie Lydia Megert, Bern, Switzerland. 1983 Leicester Polytechnic; Galerie Artek, Helsinki and touring to Galerie Blanche, Stockholm and Galerie Nordenhake, Malmo. 1984 Waddington Galleries Ltd, London. 1987 Annely Juda Fine Art, London (with Mary Martin). Died in London 1984.

56 Chance Order Change I (15 colours) 1976
oil on canvas
121.9 × 121.9 cm

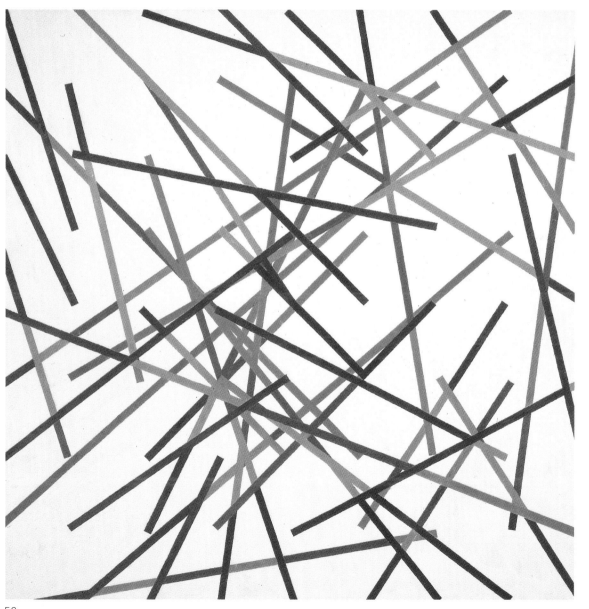

Mary Martin

Born 1907 in Folkestone, Kent. 1925-29 Studied at Goldsmiths' School of Art. 1929-32 Studied at the Royal College of Art. 1930 Married Kenneth Martin. 1944 Birth of first son John. 1946 Birth of second son Paul. 1950 First abstract paintings. 1951 First reliefs. 1954 Heffer Gallery, Cambridge (with Kenneth Martin). 1955 'Nine Abstract Artists' Redfern Gallery, London. 1956 Whitechapel Art Gallery, London *Environment* for 'This is Tomorrow' exhibition. 'Contemporary Sculpture' Hanover Gallery, London. 1957 Screen for Musgrove Park Hospital, Belfast. 1960 Institute of Contemporary Arts, London; 'Konkrete Kunst' Helmhaus, Zurich; maquettes for six reliefs 'Tidal Movements' 1-6 for the S.S. Oriana, Peninsular and Oriental Steam Navigation Company. 1961 'British Constructivist Art' American Federation of Arts, New York and tour; wall construction for the Sixth International Union of Architects Congress Headquarters, London. 1962 'Experiment in Constructie' Stedelijk Museum, Amsterdam; 'Kompas 2: hedendaagse schilderkunst uit London', Stedelijk van Abbemuseum, Eindhoven. 1963 'Construction England' Arts Council of Great Britain, London and tour. 1964 Molton and Lords Gallery, London; 'Britische Malerei der Gegenwart' Kunstverein für die Rheinlande und Westfalen: 'London Group 1914-64' Tate Gallery, London and tour. 1965 'British Sculpture in the Sixties' Tate Gallery, London; Tokyo Biennale; maquette for the Fountain at British Petroleum House, London. 1967 'ROSC '67' Dublin; 'Recent British Painting: Peter Stuyvesant Foundation Collection' Tate Gallery, London. 1968 Axiom Gallery, London. 1969 Nuremberg Biennale; wall construction for the University of Stirling. 1970 Museum of Modern Art, Oxford and tour (with Kenneth Martin); '3—00: New Multiple Art' Whitechapel Art Gallery, London. 1974 'Basically White' Institute of Contemporary Arts, London. 1977 'Series' Tate Gallery, London. 1980 'Pier + Ocean' Hayward Gallery, London. 1981 'British Sculpture in the 20th Century. Part 2' Whitechapel Art Gallery, London. 1984 The Tate Gallery, London. 1987 Annely Juda Fine Art, London (with Kenneth Martin). 1969 Died in London.

57 Compound Rhythms 1966
painted wood and stainless steel on wood and formica
108 × 108 × 11.4 cm

John McLaughlin

Born 1898 in Sharon, Massachusetts. Self-taught, travelled widely in Japan and the Far East studying language and art between 1935 and 1940 and during the Second World War he was an intelligence officer in China, Burma and India. He won the Tamarind Lithography Fellowship, Los Angeles in 1963 and the Visual Arts Award, National Endowment for the Arts, Washington D.C. in 1967. His first one-man show was with the Felix Landau Gallery, Los Angeles in 1953 and he subsequently had regular shows there. Other one-man exhibitions include the University of California, Riverside 1958; Long Beach Museum of Art, California 1960; 'Retrospective' at the Pasadena Art Museum, California 1963; Corcoran Gallery, Washington D.C. 1969; Nicholas Wilder Gallery, Los Angeles 1972; 'Retrospective' La Jolla Museum of Contemporary Art, California 1973; Whitney Museum of American Art, New York and André Emmerich Gallery, New York in 1974 and 1979; Felicity Samuel Gallery, London 1975; Galerie André Emmerich, Zurich 1976; Nicholas Wilder Gallery, Los Angeles 1979; Annely Juda Fine Art, London 1981; Gatodo Gallery, Tokyo 1983, 1984 and 1985. His work has been exhibited in numerous group shows, including 'Pacific Coast Art' which toured the Cincinnati Art Museum, San Francisco Museum of Art, Walker Art Center, Minneapolis 1955 and 'Four Abstract Classicists' which was shown at the Los Angeles County Museum; San Francisco Museum; I.C.A. London and Queens College, Belfast 1959-60. In 1962 'Geometric Abstraction in America', Whitney Museum of Art, New York which was a touring exhibition; 1965 'The Responsive Eye', Museum of Modern Art, New York; 1971 '11 Los Angeles Artists', Hayward Gallery, London (toured Britain) and in 1975 the international travelling exhibition 'Color as Language', Museum of Modern Art, New York. Amongst the public collections he is represented in are the Metropolitan Museum of Art and the Museum of Modern Art in New York; the Smithsonian Institute and the Corcoran Gallery of Art in Washington D.C.; the County Museum of Art, Los Angeles; Museum of Modern Art, Pasadena; University of California, Berkeley and the Wadsworth Atheneum Connecticut. 1976 Died in California.

58 Untitled 1974/75
acrylic on canvas
122 × 152 cm

Robert Michel

1897 Born in Vockenhausen/Taunus. End of First World War moved to Weimar. 1918-19 Own studio in Weimar. 1919 Married Ella Bergmann in October. 1920 Moved with her to Schmelzmühle, Vockenhausen, the family house. Until 1923 exhibitions with Galerie von Garvens, Hanover also Karl Nierendorf, Cologne and later, Berlin. 1923 and 1925 Exhibited at Nassauischer Kunstverein, Wiesbaden with El Lissitzky and Kurt Schwitters. 1926 Became member of the group 'The New Frankfurt'. 1927 Travelled with Schwitters in Holland. 1928 Travelling exhibition 'Societé Anonyme' U.S.A. 1930 'International Exhibition for Art of Advertising' Essen. 1932 'Abstract Art' Frankfurt and B.D.A. exhibition 'Cheap Houses for Fixed Prices' Frankfurt. 1933 'Building and Living' Frankfurt. Member of the Association of German Architects. 1933-45 No artistic work. Involved in fisheries and economic waterplanning. 1960-62 Lords Gallery, London; Gallery Delta, Basle. 1963 'Pioneers of the Collage' Schloss Morsbroich, Leverkusen. 1964 'Cinquante ans de Collage' Musée St. Etienne and Paris; 'Was da ist' Galerie Loehr, Frankfurt-Niederursel. 1967 Gulbenkian Gallery, Newcastle; 'Collage '67' Städtische Galerie im Lenbachhaus, Munich. 1968 'Collage to Assemblage' Institute for Modern Art, Nuremberg; 50 Year Retrospective, Waddell Gallery, New York; 'Collagen aus sechs jarhzehnten' Frankfurt Kunstverein and Kunstgewerbemuseum, Zurich. 1969 Queen's Gallery, Belfast; 'Industrie und Technik' Wilhelm-Lehmbruck-Museum, Duisburg and Poland. 1970 'Ella Bergmann-Michel + Robert Michel, Collagen' Stadthaus, Paderborn; 'The Non-Objective World 1914-1924' Annely Juda Fine Art, London. 1971 Retrospective Exhibition, Galerie Loehr, Frankfurt-Niederursel and Werkbund-Haus, Dusseldorf; 'The Non-Objective World 1924-1939' Annely Juda Fine Art, London; Galleria Milano, Milan; Galerie Jean Chauvelin, Paris and Galerie Liatowitsch, Basle. 'Deutsche Avantgarde' Galerie Gmurzynska-Bargera, Cologne. 1972 Retrospective Exhibition 1917-1966, Annely Juda Fine Art, London; 'The Non-Objective World 1939-1955' Annely Juda Fine Art, London. 1973 'The Non-Objective World 1914-1955' Annely Juda Fine Art, London. 1974 Retrospective, Kunsthalle, Hamburg; Retrospective, Galerie Bargera, Cologne. 1977 Galerie Loehr, Frankfurt-Niederursel; Permanent Loan to Stadhaus, Paderborn. 1978 'The Non-Objective World 1914-1939' Annely Juda Fine Art, London. 1980 'Abstraction 1910-1940' Annely Juda Fine Art, London; Kulturkreis, Eppstein. 1982 'Robert Michel: Collages 1918-1930' Annely Juda Fine Art, London. 1983 Died Titisee-Neustadt, W. Germany.

59 Für Hans Grade! 1921
ink and colour wash on paper
collaged on card
65 × 85 cm
titled lower left

60 Entresol für E8 II 1928
ink, wash and silver paint
56 × 84.5 cm
titled top left, initialled and dated lower right

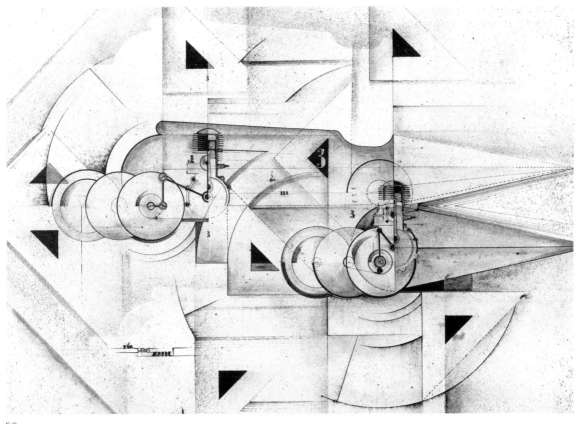

Laszlo Moholy-Nagy

Born 1895 in Bacsbarod (Hungary). Studied law in Budapest. 1914-1917 Military service. In 1917 he started to paint. One of the group of artists associated with Lajos Kassak and the magazine 'Ma' (Today). 1918 Finished studies in Budapest. Devoted himself entirely to painting influenced by Malevich and El Lissitzky. 1919-1920 In Vienna, contact with the Dada group. Published 'Book of the New Artists' with Kassak in Vienna. 1921 In Berlin, met Lissitzky and Schwitters. Connections with Herwarth Walden. 1922 Exhibition at the 'Der Sturm' gallery in Berlin. Took part in the constructivist congress organised by van Doesburg in Weimar. 1923 Invited by Walter Gropius to the Bauhaus, Weimar. Taught at the Bauhaus, took over Itten's preparatory course and Klee's metal workshop. Typographic and photographic experiments. 1925 Moved with the Bauhaus to Dessau. Edited the Bauhaus books together with Walter Gropius. 1928 Left the Bauhaus and settled in Berlin. Stage design for the Kroll Opera and the Piscator Theatre. First experiments with films. Construction of film modulators. 1930 Exhibited the light-machine at the International Werkbund Exhibition in Paris. 1934 Emigrated to Amsterdam. 1935 in London. 1937 Founded the 'New Bauhaus' in Chicago. 1938 Founded the 'New School of Design'. Continued painting and industrial design. Died 1946 in Chicago. Moholy-Nagy worked in almost every medium of the plastic arts: painting, collage, typography, design, film, photography, experimentation in light and colour, stage design.

61 RU 1946
tempera on paper laid down on board
36.5 × 50 cm
signed right side

Henry Moore

Born 1898 at Castleford, Yorkshire. 1919 Entered Leeds School of Art. 1921 Awarded scholarship to Royal College of Art, London. 1926 Carved the first of the reclining figures. 1930 Moved to Hampstead where Hepworth, Nicholson and Gabo also lived. 1946 First visit to the United States. 1948 Awarded the International Sculpture Prize at Venice Biennale. 1963 Appointed member of the Order of Merit. 1972 Retrospective exhibition at Forte di Belvedere, Florence. 1973 Awarded the Premio Umberto Biancamano, Milan. 1974 Opening of the Henry Moore Sculpture Centre at the Art Gallery of Ontario, Toronto. 1975 Awarded the Kaiserring der Stadt Goslar, West Germany. 1977 Formed the Henry Moore Foundation. 1978 Major donation of sculptures to the Tate Gallery, London; eightieth birthday exhibitions at the Serpentine Gallery and in Kensington Gardens, London and the City Art Gallery, Bradford. 1980 Donation of 'Large Arch' to the Department of the Environment for permanent siting in Kensington Gardens, London. 1981 Retrospective exhibition in Madrid. 1986 Retrospective exhibition in Hongkong and Tokyo. Died at Much Hadham, Hertfordshire.

62 Sculptural Forms   1935
pastel
38.7 × 52.1 cm
signed and dated lower right

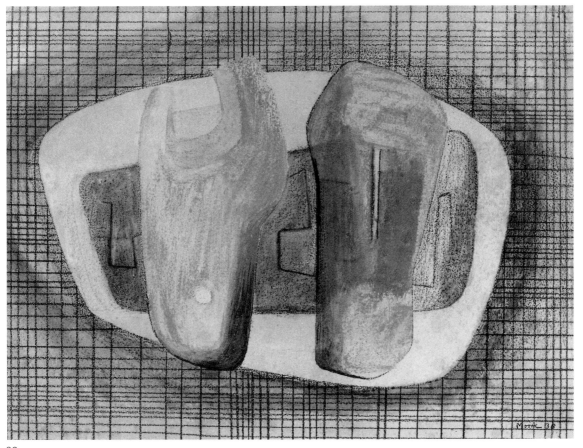

Francois Morellet

1926 Born in Cholet, France. 1945-47 Studied at the Ecole de Langues Orientaux, Paris (Degree in Russian). 1948-75 General Manager at the Morellet-Guerineau toy and pram factory, Cholet. 1950-51 Travelled in Brazil, met the artist Alvir Mavignier. 1952 Travelled in Spain. 1954 In Switzerland and Germany, met Max Bill. 1960-68 Co-founder with Sobrino, Le Parc, Stein, Yvaral and Rossi of the Groupe de Recherche d'Art Visuel, Paris. 1960-62 Travelled in the U.S.A. His one-man exhibitions include: 1950 Galerie Creuze, Paris. 1958 Galerie Colette Allendy, Paris. 1960 Galerie Aujourd'hui, Brussels. 1966 Galerie Der Spiegel, Cologne. 1967 Galerie Denise René, rive droite et rive gauche, Paris; Galerie Indica, London. 1969 Galerie Swart, Amsterdam. 1970 Galerie m, Bochum; Galerie Denise René & Hans Mayer, Dusseldorf; Galerie Swart, Amsterdam. 1971 Galerie La Bertesca, Genoa; Stedelijk Van Abbemuseum, Eindhoven; C.N.A.C., Paris; Galerie Denise René, rive gauche, Paris; Kunstverein, Hamburg; Schloss Morsbroich, Leverkusen; Galerie m, Bochum; Kunstverein, Frankfurt; 1972 Palais des Beaux-Arts, Brussels; Kunstmuseum, Bochum; Lucy Milton Gallery, London; Musée des Beaux-Arts, Grenoble (With Roman Cieslewicz); Kunstmuseum Dusseldorf; 1972-74 Travelling exhibitions organised by C.N.A.C., Paris, shown at 18 museums and 'maisons de la culture' in France. 1973 Musée des Beaux-Arts, Nantes; Galerie Arte Contacto, Caracas; Galerie Swart, Amsterdam; Galerie D + C Mueller-Roth, Stuttgart. 1974 Lucy Milton Gallery, London; Galerie Lydia Megert, Berne; Galerie Cavallino, Venice; Kunsthalle, Bielefeld. 1974-75 Travelling exhibitions organised by Lucy Milton Gallery, London; shown at 11 museums in England. 1976 Studio Marconi, Milan; Galerie m, Bochum and The Hague; Galerie Swart, Amsterdam. 1976 Galerie D + C Mueller-Roth, Stuttgart; Westfälischer Kunstverein, Munster. 1977 Nationalgalerie, Berlin; Staatliche Kunsthalle, Baden-Baden; Musée. d'Art Moderne de la ville de Paris; Kunsthalle, Kiel; Annely Juda Fine Art, London; Galerie Swart, Amsterdam; Galerie Gillespie-De Laage, Paris. 1978 Galerie Lydia Megert, Berne; Galerie Gillespie-De Laage, Paris; Studio Marconi, Milan; Musée d'Art Moderne de la ville de Paris. 1979 Galerie Swart, Amsterdam; Galerie Le Coin du Miroir, Dijon; Galerie D + C Mueller-Roth, Stuttgart; Galerie Nordenhake, Malmö; Musée de Beaux-Arts, Toulon; Galerie m, Bochum. 1981 Helsingin Kaupungin Taidemuseo, Helsinki; Galerie Gilles Gheerbrant, Montréal; Annely Juda Fine Art, London. Numerous museum exhibitions since. Lives and works in France.

63 Seule droite traversant 2 carrés dans 2 plans différents 1978
acrylic on canvas, 2 parts
overall size: 43.5 × 83.5 cm

Antoine Pevsner

Born January 18, 1886 in Orel, Russia. Studied art at Kiev and St. Petersburg. In Paris, saw Cubist pictures in the Salon des Indépendants in 1911, and the exhibition of Boccioni's sculpture at the Galerie de la Boétie in 1913. Knew Archipenko and Modigliani. Spent the war years in Oslo with his brother Naum Gabo. 1917 Returned to Russia and was appointed professor in the Wchutemas (Higher Art and Technical Workshop) along with Tatlin and Malevich. 1920 With Gabo signed the Realist Manifesto. 1922 Exhibited Constructivist sculptures in the Soviet government-sponsored exhibition in the Galerie van Diemen, Berlin. 1923 In the face of official opposition to his views on art, moved to Berlin, then to Paris. 1924 Exhibited with Gabo at the Galerie Percier in Paris. Three years later they collaborated on designs for Diaghilev's ballet *La Chatte*. 1931 A founder member of Abstraction-Création, Paris. From 1946 to 1952 active in Salon des Réalités Nouvelles. Work seen in numerous exhibitions in the 1940s and 1950s, including the Venice Biennale and the Brussels World's Fair of 1958. Died April 12, 1962 in Paris.

64 Composition 1923
encaustic on copper
41.5 × 30 cm
dated lower left, signed lower right

Serge Poliakoff

Born in Moscow 1906. 1919 Emigrated and travelled in Europe. 1923 Settled in Paris where he earned his living as a guitarist. 1930 Studied at Academie Frochot, Grande Chaumière. 1935 Regularly worked at the Slade School. 1937 In Paris. Met Kandinsky. 1938 Regularly attended meeting of artists at the studio of Sonia and Robert Delaunay. 1945 First one-man show at L'Esquisse Gallery. 1947 Kandinsky Prize. 1952 Impressed by the work of Malevich. 1953 One-man show at the Palais des Beaux-Arts in Brussels. 1956 Received Lissone Prize. 1957 Kunsthalle, Hamburg. 1958 Kunshalle, Dusseldorf; Statens Museum for Kunst, Copenhagen; Hanover Gallery, London; Carnegie International, Pittsburg, U.S.A. 1959 Documenta 11, Kassel. 1960 Kunsthalle, Berne. 1962 Became a French citizen and settled in the Alpes Maritimes. 1968 Retrospective at the Maison de la Culture, Caen. 1969 Visited Venice and Padua. Had a Retrospective at the Musée de Mont-de-Marsan. Awards: 1938 Prix de la Piste a l'Ecran, Galerie Ceunere, Paris. 1947 Kandinsky Prize, Paris. 1956 Premio Lissone, Italy. 1962 Commandeur des Arts et des Lettres, Paris. 1965 International Prize, Tokyo Biennale. 1966 Grand Prix, Menton Biennale. 1969 Died in Paris.

65 Composition Abstraite, noir, rouge, gris, bleu
1965-66
oil on canvas
92 × 73 cm
signed lower right

Liubov Popova

Born 1889 near Moscow. 1907-1908 Attended the studios of Stanislav Zhukovsky and Konstantin Yuon in Moscow. Late 1900s made many trips to ancient Russian cities such as Pskov and Vologda, studying Russian church architecture and art. 1910 Travelled to Italy where she was especially impressed by Giotto. 1912 Worked in the Moscow studio known as 'The Tower' together with Viktor Bart, Tatlin and Kirill Zdanevich. 1912-1913 Worked in Paris, frequenting the studios of Le Fauconnier and Metzinger. Met Vera Pestel and Nadezhda Udaltsova there. 1913 Returned to Russia. Again worked close to Tatlin and also Udaltsova and Alexandr Vesnin. 1914 Travelled to France and Italy again. 1914-1916 Contributed to the 'Jack of Diamonds' (Moscow, 1914 and 1916), 'Tramway V', 'O.10' and 'The Store'. 1915-1921 Painted in a non-objective style. 1916-1918 Painted 'architectonic compositions'. 1919-1921 Painted 'painterly constructions'. 1918 Professor at Svomas/Vkhutemas. 1919 Contributed to the Xth State Exhibition 'Non-Objective Creation and Suprematism' and other exhibitions thereafter. 1920 Member of Inkhuk. 1921 Took part in '5 x 5 = 25'; rejected studio painting and experimented with design in various fields including book design, porcelain, textiles and dresses. 1922 Created set and costume designs for Mierkhold's production of Crommelynck's farce 'The Magnanimous Cuckold'. 1922 Contributed to the 'Erste Russische Kunstaustellung' in Berlin. 1923 Designed sets and costumes for Sergei Tretiakov's 'Earth in Turmoil'. 1923-24 Worked on dress and textile designs for the First State Textile Factory, Moscow. Died 1924 in Moscow. 1924 Posthumous exhibition in Moscow.

66 Composition *c.* 1920-21
gouache on card
67.5 × 53.5 cm

67 Untitled 1922-23
oil and gesso on canvas
72 × 72 cm

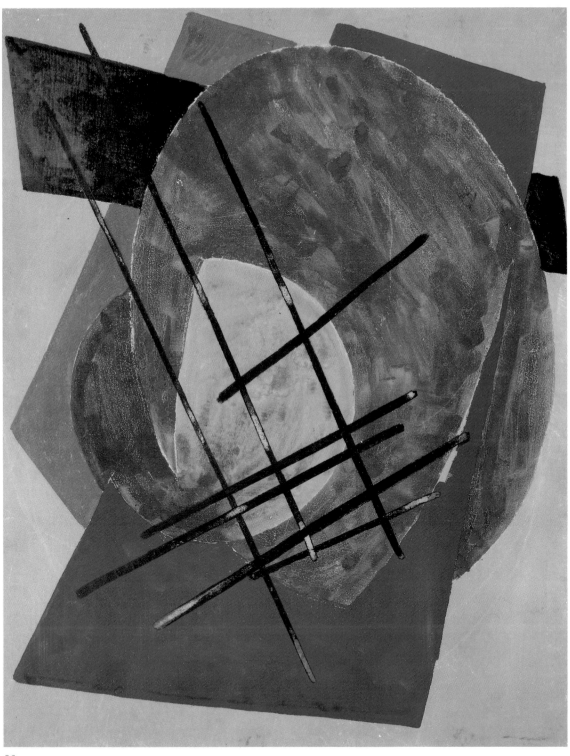

Alan Reynolds

Born 1926 in Newmarket, Suffolk. From 1948 to 1952
he studied at Woolwich Polytechnic School of Art and in
1952 was awarded a scholarship to the Royal College of
Art. Between 1954 and 1961 he taught drawing at the
Central School of Arts & Crafts in London and has been
teaching at St. Martin's School of Art since 1961, where
he is now Associate Lecturer of Painting. Until 1958 he
painted landscapes. From then until 1966 he did
abstract paintings and watercolours with emphasis on
pictorial construction and in 1969 constructed his first
group of reliefs in painted wood, curvilinear in form
which were influenced by the work of Sophie Täuber-
Arp. In 1975 he began making constructional reliefs,
orthogonal in form and the following year he went on to
free-standing, painted wood constructions. In 1978 he
started doing modular constructions and drawings. He
has had ten one-man exhibitions at the Redfern Gallery,
London during the 1950's, the 60's and early 70's. Also
at the Durlacher Gallery, New York in 1954 and 1958;
Leicester Galleries, London 1958; Annely Juda Fine Art,
London 1978; Galerie Renée Zeigler, Zurich 1980; Juda
Rowan Gallery, London 1982 and 1984; Galerie Wack,
Kaiserslautern 1986. Among the group exhibitions he
has participated in are the Pittsburgh International in
1952, 1955, 1958 and 1961; 'International Water-
colour Exhibition' Brooklyn 1953. In 1955 he took part in
several group shows at the Musée National d'Art Moderne in Paris; Palais des Beaux Arts in Brussels and the
British Council exhibition 'British Contemporary Painting'
in Oslo and Copenhagen. 1957 and 1960 'Critic's
Choice' Arthur Tooth and Sons London. 1971 'Spectrum
Exhibition' Arts Council of Great Britain and 'British Painting 1952-77' at the Royal Academy, London. 1977
Galerie Loyse Oppenheim, Nyon, Switzerland. 1980
'Eight + Eight' Annely Juda Fine Art London. His work is
represented in numerous British public collections
including the Arts Council, British Council, Tate Gallery
and Victoria & Albert Museum, London and in inter-
national collections such as the Museum of Modern Art,
New York; The Cleveland Museum of Art; the National
Gallery of Canada in Ottawa; the Musée d'Art, Grenoble;
Museum Pfalzgalerie Kaiserslautern; the Wilhelm-Hack
Museum, Lugwigshafen and in Australia the National
Galleries in Adelaide, Melbourne and Sydney. He lives
and works in Kent.

68 Structures – Group II (16)   1987
prepared card on wood base
140 × 93 cm
signed, titled and dated on verso

Georges Ribemont-Dessaignes

1884 Born at Montpellier on the 19th June. 1904 Studied in the studio of J. P. Laurens then, for a short while at the Académie Julian. 1909 Met the three Duchamp brothers – Raymond Duchamp-Villon, Jaques Villon and Marcel Duchamp. Helped them organise meetings with such artists as Puteaux, Leger, Metzinger, Gleizes and sometimes Picabia. Member of the Société des Indépendants and then associate of the Salon d'Automne. Helped to found La Section d'Or. 1914-18 During the war worked in administration, stopped painting and began to write poetry. 1918 Wrote L'Empereur de Chine, which was published a few years later in the Collection dada. 1918 With Picabia, who had returned from the U.S., went to Zurich and met Tristan Tzara. Became involved with Dada, collaborating in all their publications: Dada, 391, Littérature, Z, Die Schammade (Cologne), Dada Almanach (Berlin), Mecano (Leyde). Took part in all their 'happenings'. Probably influenced by Picabia's new style of painting he began painting again and had an exhibition in Paris, with a catalogue introduction by Tristan Tzara and another in Geneva, organised by Serner. 1922 Opposed the Congrès de Paris along with Eluard, Satie and Tzara. Worked on the pamphlet Le Couer à Barbe. 1929 After the review Le Grand Jeu broke completely with Breton and the Surrealist group with whom he had associated for a while. Died in 1974.

69 L'Esprit Oceanique   1918
mechanical oil painting
100 × 81 cm
initialled and titled lower left

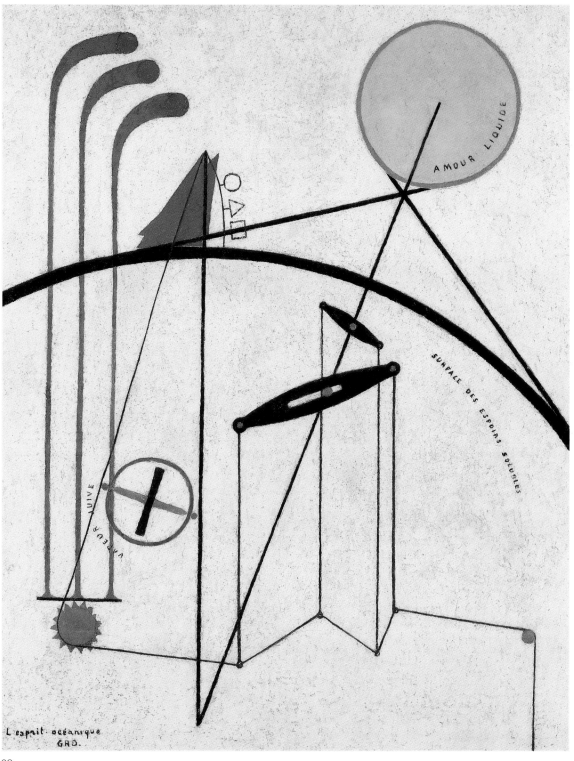

AMOUR LIQUIDE

SURFACE DES ESPOIRS SOLUBLES

VAPEUR LUIVE

L'esprit océanique
GRO.

Kurt Schwitters

1887 Born in Hanover. 1909-1914 Studied in Hanover, Dresden and Berlin. 1918 First abstract painting. Exhibition at the Gallery 'Der Sturm' Berlin. Developed the idea of Merz-painting, as a special form of the Dada movement, Merz publications. 1920 Exhibited at the 'Societé Anonymye' in New York. Published 'Die Wahrheit über Anna Blume' (The Truth about Anna Blume). Plastic work: the 'Merz' house. At first, the Dadaists of Berlin refused to work with him because of his collaboration with the 'Sturm'. Lectured in Prague. 1921 Contact with Raoul Hausmann, who influenced Schwitters in experiments with sound-poetry 'Lautgedichte'. 1922 Visited the Dada Congress in Weimar. Together with Theo van Doesburg and his wife took part in Dada events in Holland. Co-operation with the leading avantgarde magazines. 1924 Friendship with Theo van Doesburg and El Lissitzky during their stay in Hanover. Foundation of Merz publishing house and publication of the Merz-series. Opened a studio for advertising design. As early as 1920 he built the famous Merzbau in Hanover. 1932 Member of the group 'Abstraction-Création' in Paris. 1933 Short stay in Norway. 1937 Left Germany. 1940 Flight to England. 1941-1945 In England. Continuation of the Merz-painting. Third Merzbau. 1948 Died in Ambleside. 1985-86 Major retrospective exhibition at the Museum of Modern Art, New York; Tate Gallery, London; Sprengel Museum, Hanover.

70 Untitled   1942
collage mounted on card
collage: 16 × 16 cm
signed, dated and inscribed on mount

Kurt Schwitters 1942
für Meta

Nicholas de Stael

1914 Born St. Petersburg, Russia. 1922-30 Studied at Jesuit College de Saint Michel, Brussels. 1932-34 Studied at the Academie Saint Gilles and the Academie Royal des Beaux-Arts, Brussels (with Prof. van Haelen). 1933-37 Travelled in the Netherlands, France, Spain, Morocco, Italy and Algeria. 1938-41 Lived in Paris. 1938 Worked with Fernand Leger at the Academie Libre, Paris. 1940 Served in the French Foreign Legion, Tunisia. 1941 Destroyed most pre-1940 work. 1941-43 Lived in Nice, France. Associated with Magnelli, Jean Klein, Marie Raymond, Robert and Sonia Delaunay and Le Corbusier. 1943 Returned to Paris. Associated with Braque and Lanskoy. 1948 Acquired French nationality. 1949 Travelled in the Netherlands and Belgium. 1950 In London. 1952 Painted in Normandy and the Seine Valley, France. Worked on ballet projects with Rene Clair and Piette Lecuire, Paris. 1953 Travelled in Italy and New York. 1954 Moved to Antibes, France. 1955 Committed suicide in Antibes.

71 Paysage CR 331   1952
oil on card
24 × 33 cm
signed on verso

72 Paysage CR 640   1953
oil on canvas
24 × 33 cm
signed on verso

Henryk Stazewski

1894 Born in Warsaw. 1913-19 Studied at the Warsaw
Academy of Fine Art. 1923 Cubist and purist paintings.
Took part in an exhibition of New Art in Wilna. First
manifestation of the Constructivist Avantgarde in Poland
(Strzeminski, Szczuka, Zarnower). 1924 Co-founder of
the group 'Blok' which united the entire Polish
Avantgarde (Strzeminski, Kobro, Szczuka, Zarnower,
Berlewi, Stazewski). One of the editors of 'Blok' (Nos. 1-
5). 1925 Travelled to Paris. First contact with Mondrian
and Seuphor. 1926 Dissolution of the group and of
'Blok'. Co-founder of the group 'Praesens' which united
architects and painters. Stazewski was the editor for
painting. 1929 Abstract geometric compostions.
Travelled to Italy and Paris. Left 'Praesens' and founded a
new group 'a.r.'. Member of the group 'Cercle et Carré'.
1933 Exhibited with Krynski at the Institute of Propaganda, Warsaw. 1934 One-man show with
Strzeminski of landscapes and portraits. Worked a lot
with typography. 1939-45 No paintings. His house in
Warsaw was bombed and all his works were destroyed.
Only a few paintings in the Museum in Lodz and private
collections abroad were rescued. 1957 Compositions
hovering between painting and flat reliefs. 1958 White
reliefs. 1960 and 1962 Exhibitions at Galerie Krzywego
Kola, Warsaw. 1963 Exhibition at the Grabowski Gallery,
London. 1964 Reliefs in metal, polished aluminium and
copper. Exhibited at the Kazimir Gallery, Chicago. 1965
Participated in the Biennale at Elblag and had an exhibi-
tion at Zacheta, Warsaw. 1966 Worked with the Galerie
Foksal in Warsaw. Exhibited at the Kazimir Gallery,
Chicago and the XXXIII Biennale di Venezia (menzione
d'onore). 1967 Exhibited at Galeria Foksal, Warsaw and
the Musée des Beaux-Arts, La Chaux-de-Fond. 1968
Exhibited at the Galeria Mona Lisa, Wroclaw. 1969
Exhibited at the Galeria Foksal, Warsaw and the Museum
Sztuki, Lodz. 1970 Realised the unlimited vertical com-
position entitled '9 light rays in the sky' at the Sym-
posium, Warsaw 70. Also exhibited at the Narodni
Galerie, Prague. 1972 Won the J. G. Herder Prize. 1975
System paintings and geometric analysis of the pain-
tings by George de La Tour and other Baroque painters.
1977 Exhibited at Galerie Teufel, Köln. 1978 Exhibited at
Zacheta, Warsaw. 1979 Took part in the exhibition
'L'Avanguardia Polacca 1910-1978' which toured to
Rome, Venice, Edinburgh, Glasgow and Warsaw. 1980
Exhibited at the Moderne Galerie-Quadrat Bottrop.
1982 Exhibited at Annely Juda Fine Art, London.
Stazewski has also exhibited in numerous international
group exhibitions and is included in many public and
private collections. He lives and works in Warsaw.

73 Composition No. 80   1976
oil on board
44 × 44 cm
signed, titled and dated on verso

74 Untitled   1980
oil on board
44 × 44 cm
signed and dated on verso

Nikolay Suetin

Born 1897. 1918-1922 Studied at the Vitebsk Art Institute under Malevich. 1922 Followed Malevich to Leningrad where he continued his studies under him and collaborated with him in the theoretical section of the Institute of Artistic Culture. Began work as a designer at the Lomonosov State Porcelain Factory in Petrograd with Malevich and Chashnik. 1924-1926 Was affiliated with Ginkhuk and worked with Malevich on architectural constructions ('arkhitektony' and 'planity'). During the late 1920s Suetin developed his own theory of art. 1932 Appointed artistic director of the Lomonosov Factory where he remained until 1952. 1937 Helped design the Soviet pavilion at the Exposition Internationale, Paris, for which he received a Grand Prix. 1939 In charge of the Soviet pavilion for the New York World's Fair. 1954 Died in Leningrad.

75 Architectural Study *c.* 1922-23
ink on paper
27.9 × 26.8 cm

76 Suprematist Coffee-Pot 1923
hand-painted porcelain
height: 16 cm
signed and inscribed in Russian

77 Cup and Saucer
porcelain
height: 6 cm
diameter: 15.2 cm

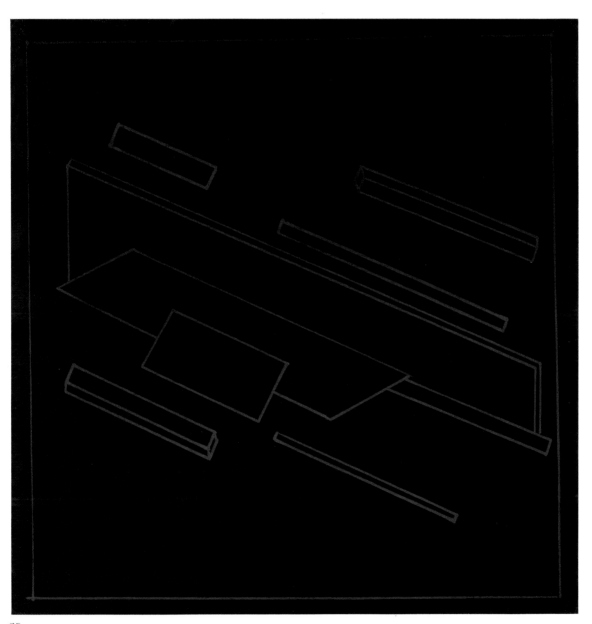

Vladimir Tatlin

Born 1885 in Kharkow (Russia). Art School in Pensa. Merchant Navy until 1909. Studies from 1909-1911 at the school for painting, sculpture and architecture Moscow. Shared studio with Alexandr Vesnin. Friendship with Michael Larionov. 1913 Travelled via Berlin to Paris to visit Picasso. Showed 1915 his first 'Contre-Reliefs' in Petrograd. Designed 1917 with Georgi Jakulov the 'Café Pittoresque' in Moscow. After the Revolution 1918 Tatlin became director of all artist organizations. Lectureships at the new Art Schools. 1922 Design and execution of the model for the tower III International in Petrograd. 1926-1927 Lived in Kiev. Worked in Moscow on WCHUTEIN. Design and development of industrial products. Beginning of the thirties designs and models for gliders. 'Letatlin'. Since 1933 stage designer in Moscow. Returned to traditional painting. Died 1953 in Moscow.

78 Reconstruction of Tatlin 'Painting Relief 1913-14'
reconstructed by Martyn Chalk 1982
wood, paper, pencil, gouache, wallpaper etc
60.5 × 29.2 × 6.6 cm

79 Reconstruction of Tatlin 'Painting Relief 1913-14'
reconstructed by Martyn Chalk 1982
wood, paper, gouache, oil paint, card etc
70 × 40 × 6 cm

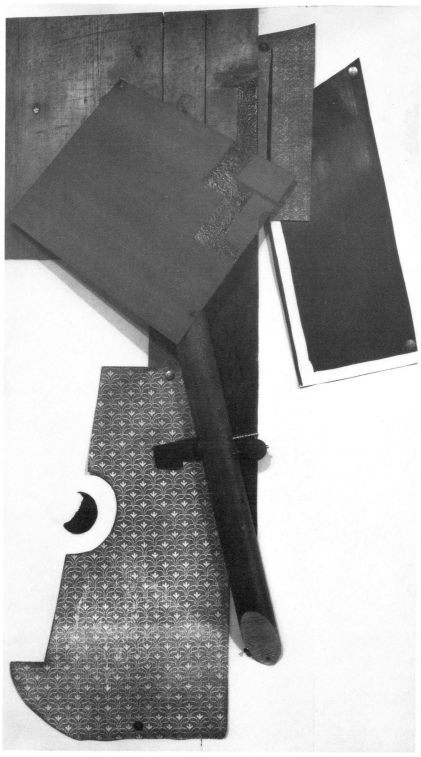

Georges Vantongerloo

Born 1886 in Antwerp. Studied at the academies in Antwerp and Brussels. 1916 Meeting with van Doesburg. 1917-22 Co-signs the first manifesto of the 'De Stijl' art group and collaborator of the journal 'De Stijl'. 1917 First abstract works. 1919-27 Lived in Menton. 1922 Exposition Internationale de l'art d'Aujourdhui, Geneva. 1927 Moved to Paris. Correspondence with Mr. Jaspar, Prime Minister concerning project made for a bridge for l'Escaut, Antwerp. 1929 Graphisches Kabinett, Munich; 'Abstrakte und Surrealistische Malerei und Plastik' Kunsthaus Zurich. 1930 'Cercle et Carré' Galerie 23, Paris; Aeroclub de France, Pavillon Marsan, Paris; International Exhibition, Stockholm. 1931 Foundation member of 'Abstraction-Création' and vice-president of the group until 1937. 1934 Galerie Abstraction-Création, Paris. 1935 L'art mural, Paris. 1936 Salon des Surindependants, Paris; 'Cubism and Abstract Art' Museum of Modern Art, New York. 1937 'Konstruktivisten' Kunsthalle Basle; use of circular line. 1938 'Abstract Art' Stedelijk Museum, Amsterdam. 1939 'Art Non-Objectiv' Galerie Charpentier, Paris. 1943 Galerie de Berri, Paris. 1946 Salon des Réalités Nouvelles, Paris. 1947 'Arte Astratta e Concreta' Palazzo Ex-Reale, Milan. 1949 Exhibited together with Max Bill and Antoine Pevsner in Kunsthaus, Zurich. 1950 'Europäische Kunst 13-20 Jahrhundert aus Züricher Sammlungen' Kunsthaus Zurich; Sidney Janis Gallery, New York. 1951 'Max Bill, Julius Bissier, Georges Vantongerloo' Kunstverein Freiburg. 1953 Galleria Origine, Rome; Rose Fried Gallery, New York. 1960 'Konkrete Kunst – 50 Jahre Entwicklung' Helmhaus Zurich. 1961 'II Expostion Internationale de Sculpture' Musée Rodin, Paris. 1962 Marlborough Fine Art, London. 1965 Died in Paris.

80 Attraction-Répulsion   Paris 1954
oil
50 × 92 cm

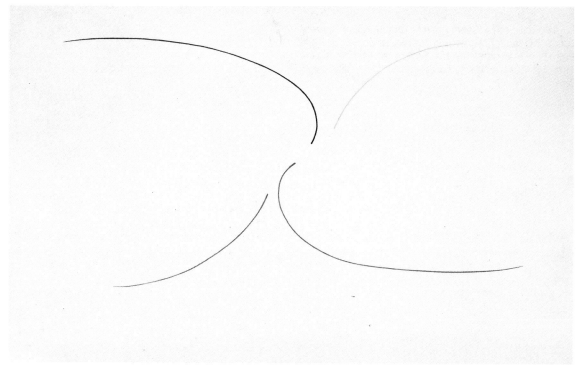

Paule Vezelay

Born 1893 in England. 1912-1914 Studied at Slade School of Fine Art for short period; then studied under George Belcher, R.A., for two years. First became known as a book illustrator, lithographer and wood engraver. 1920 First visit to Paris. 1921 First one-man exhibition Gallery Dorian Leigh, London. Invited to become member of the London Group. 1926 Settled in Paris. 1928 First non-figurative works. 1929-1939 Member of 'Les Artistes des Sur-Indépendants'. 1934 Invited to join 'Abstraction-Création' with Arp, Täuber-Arp, Herbin and others. 1936 Invented first construction in wire and threads in space. 1938 Exhibited at Galleria del Millione, Milan, with Arp, Domela, Kandinsky, Magnelli, Seligmann, Täuber-Arp and at Internationale de l'Art Non-figuratif, Gemeente Museum, Amsterdam. 1939 Exhibited Internationale de l'Art Abstrait, Galerie Charpentier, Paris. Returned to England. War years in Bristol and London. 1946 First post-war visit to Paris for her fifth exhibition at Galerie Jeanne Bucher. Member of the Salon des Réalités Nouvelles. 1953 Joined Groupe Espace. 1983 Retrospective exhibition at the Tate Gallery, London. 1984 Died in London.

81 Souvenir of a Museum 1934
charcoal on canvas
92 × 73 cm
signed lower right, dated lower left

Friedrich Vordemberge-Gildewart

1899 Born November 17 in Osnabrück. After school apprenticed to a carpenter. 1919 Studied Hanover School of Art and Technical College, Hanover (sculpture, architecture and painting). First abstract works (reliefs, design for sculpture). 1924 Studio in the house of the Kestner Gesellschaft. Formation of the group 'K' (together with Hans Nitzschke). Exhibition of the group 'K' in the Kestner Gesellschaft Hanover. Meeting with Schwitters, Arp and van Doesburg. Member of the 'Sturm' Berlin and 'de Stijl' Leiden. 1925 Exhibition in the 'Sturm'; 'L'Art d'Aujourd'hui' in Paris and the 'Great Berlin Exhibition' Lehrter Railway Station, Berlin. 1926-27 'Societé Anonyme' Brooklyn, New York. 1927 Founder member together with Kurt Schwitters and Carl Buchheister, 'The Abstracts, Hanover'. 1929 Exhibition Galerie Povolozky, Paris; 'Abstract and surrealist painting and sculpture' Kunsthaus, Zurich. 1930 Participated in the first international exhibition of 'Cercle et Carré' Paris and exhibition 'Vision and laws of form' Galerie Ferdinand Möller, Berlin. 1932 Founder member of 'Abstraction-Création' Paris. 1934 Exhibition in Milan Galleria del Milione and Rome, 'Bragaglia Fuori Commercio'. 1936 'Degenerate Art' Berlin. 1936-38 In Berlin. 1937-38 Switzerland; 'Constructivists' Basle. 1938 Moved to Amsterdam, 'Abstract Art' Stedelijk Museum, Amsterdam; 'Modern German Art' London. 1939 'Réalités Nouvelles' Galerie Charpentier, Paris. 1940 Publication of 'millimeter und geraden' (millimetres and straights) Duwaer, Amsterdam. 1942 Founder and editor of Duwaer, Amsterdam. Publication of Arp 'rire de coquille'; Kandinsky 'Il tableaux et 7 poèmes'. 1944 'Concrete Art', Kunsthalle, Basle. 1948 '3ème Salon Réalités Nouvelles' Palais des Beaux-Arts, Paris. 1949 Monograph 'Vordemberge-Gildewart' Editions Duwaer, Amsterdam; 'Les Premiers Maitres de l'art abstrait', Galerie Maeght, Paris. 1951 'De Stijl' Stedelijk Museum, Amsterdam. 1952 'De Stijl' XXVI Biennale Venice Lecture 'Colour as space-forming element in architecture'; Academie van beeldende kunsten, Rotterdam. 1953 Prize II. Biennale, Sao Paulo. 1954 Exhibition Galerie Ferdinand Möller, Cologne; Invitation to the 'Hochschule für Gestaltung' Ulm. 1955 Justus-Möser Medal of the city of Osnabrück. Participation I. Documenta, Kassel. 1956 Exhibition Kunsthaus, Zürich, 'Albers, Glarner, Vordemberge-Gildewart'. 1955-59 Exhibitions: Museum und Kunstverein, Ulm; Osthausmuseum, Hagen; Landesgewerbeanstalt, Kaiserslautern; Kunstverein, Frankfurt/Main; Staatliche Kunsthalle Baden-Baden (parallel with Ackermann, Itten, Kleint). 1957 'Painting Poets – painters making poetry' Kunstmuseum, St. Gallen. 1960 Participation exhibition 'Concrete Art, 50 years development', Helmhaus, Hanover. 1962 Participated in retrospective, 'The Twenties in Hanover'. Died in Ulm.

82 Project 1919
black ink and pencil on paper
25.2 × 36.2 cm

83 Ideas for Early Work c. 1924
gouache and soft pencil on grey paper, double-sided
26 × 10.6 cm

84 Composition No. 133 1942
oil on canvas
145 × 110 cm